IMPERIAL WAR MUSEUM REVIEW

ARTICLES ON ASPECTS OF
TWENTIETH CENTURY HISTORY
PRINCIPALLY BY THE STAFF OF
THE IMPERIAL WAR MUSEUM

PUBLISHED BY
THE TRUSTEES OF
THE IMPERIAL WAR MUSEUM
GENERAL EDITOR:
SUZANNE BARDGETT
HISTORICAL EDITOR:
PETER SIMKINS
DESIGNED BY
GRUNDY & NORTHEDGE DESIGNERS
DISTRIBUTED BY LEO COOPER
(PEN AND SWORD BOOKS LIMITED)
47 CHURCH STREET,
BARNSLEY S70 2AS
PRINTED BY
GRILLFORD
© TRUSTEES OF THE IMPERIAL
WAR MUSEUM AND THE AUTHORS 1993
BRITISH LIBRARY CATALOGUING-IN-PUBLICATION DATA
A CATALOGUE RECORD FOR THIS BOOK IS AVAILABLE
FROM THE BRITISH LIBRARY
ISBN 0 901627 99 2

Cover illustration: CRW Nevinson, *Troops Resting*, 1916, oil, 28" x 36", Department of Art, 5219

Contents

The end of the British Mandate in Palestine: reflections from the papers of John Watson, of the Forces Broadcasting Service

Joanne Buggins

Portrait of AC2 John Wells Watson, RAFVR, in a studio at No 4 Forces Broadcasting Unit, Mount Carmel, Haifa in 1947. (John Watson Papers) HU 53095

Joanne Buggins is a research assistant in the Department of Photographs.

Next time there is a peace, I shall be a conscientious objector,' wrote Aircraftsman John Watson, a young member of the Royal Air Force carrying out his national service in Palestine during the death throes of the British mandate. Watson was born in 1927 in India, where his father was a doctor with the Indian Medical Service. The family returned to England in 1929, settling in Hampshire. Educated at Winchester during the Second World War, Watson spent two formative years in the RAF, employed by the Forces Broadcasting Service, before going up to Oxford University in 1949. He was one of several thousand British military personnel caught up in the conflict in Palestine which marked the end of Britain's role as the mandatory power. The irony of the situation is pointed out by Michael Carver in his history of war since 1945:

> If Britain thought that her army was going to be able to sit back after VE Day and then VJ Day in 1945, she was going to be sadly disillusioned. As soon as war with Germany and then with Japan came to an end, indeed before [it] had done so, colonial conflicts ... were not slow to raise their heads. The most immediate and the most urgent was that of Palestine. [1]

Watson's numerous letters to his family eloquently describe the events of these years. The end of the Second World War saw the election by a huge majority of a

Labour administration in Britain. The new Prime Minister, Clement Attlee, appointed Ernest Bevin, the former Trades Union leader and war-time Secretary of State for Labour, as his Foreign Secretary. Bevin faced a daunting set of problems, of which Palestine was only one. [2] The Labour Government's Palestine Committee summarised the significance of the area in a report presented in September 1945:

> The Middle East is a region of vital consequence for Britain and the British Empire. It forms the point in the system of communications, by land, sea and air which links Britain with India, Australia and the Far East; it is also the Empire's main reservoir of oil. [3]

This idea that the Middle East was an area of 'vital consequence' was not new. Britain's interest in Palestine in particular dated back to the First World War, when it was deemed a strategically important area for the protection of the Suez Canal. Palestine was captured from the Turks in September 1918 by British forces under the command of General Sir Edmund Allenby and with assistance from Arab troops. In 1922, together with Iraq and Transjordan, Palestine was placed under British control by the League of Nations. In return for their contribution to the victory it was intimated that the Arab population would have the option of self-government in the future.

In the 1914 - 1918 period the total population of Palestine comprised less than nine per cent Jews, with the majority based in Jerusalem. The massacres of the Jews in Russia in the 1880s had stimulated the development of Zionism, the doctrine which aimed 'to establish a publicly and legally assured home for the Jewish people'.[4] This philosophy was endorsed by the British Government in the shape of the letter - often referred to as the Balfour Declaration - written by the Foreign Secretary, A J Balfour, to Lord Rothschild, a leading British Zionist Jew, at the time General Allenby captured Jerusalem in December 1917:

> His Majesty's Government views with favour the establishment in Palestine of a national home for the Jewish people, and will use its best endeavours to facilitate the achievement of this object, it being clearly understood that nothing shall be done which may prejudice the civil and religious rights of existing non-Jewish communities in Palestine.

The rise of the Nazis in Germany in the 1930s caused the influx of Jews into Palestine to triple. For many Jews, Britain was implicated in the extermination of their people during the horrific 'Final Solution' because of the Government's refusal to admit more than a fixed quota of refugees into Palestine. As the horror of the concentration camps became known to the world, the Zionists were seized with a single-minded determination to provide a refuge for survivors of the Holocaust. The indigenous Arabs in Palestine, on the other hand, felt that their civil and religious rights were being prejudiced. As expressed by an American journalist in 1947:

> The Arabs were not responsible for the persecution which has led to this emigration. They argue that it is not just that they should be compelled to pay for the sins of others by opening their country to hundreds of thousands of sufferers from European anti-Semitism. [5]

The Arab Rebellion started in 1936, beginning with a general strike which called for the cessation of all Jewish immigration, a ban on land sales to Jews and the establishment of an independent, national government. It was characterised by attacks on Jewish life and property, the bombing of urban areas and the shooting of British military personnel. The uprising ended in 1939 when it was broken by the British army.

The post-war Labour administration was confronted with the legacy of the contradictory promises made to the Arabs and Jews since 1917. The Jewish community in Palestine, the Yishuv, had high hopes of the new Government. Arthur Koestler, writing about the Labour victory of 1945 in the *New Statesman*, said:

> No party was so deeply committed to support Jewish immigration into Palestine as the Labour Party. On no fewer than eleven occasions from 1917 to 1945 the annual Labour Party Conference had reaffirmed this obligation ... In 1945 just before the Labour Government took office, this policy was once more confirmed and Hugh Dalton declared that 'it is morally wrong and politically indefensible to impose obstacles to the entry into Palestine now of any Jews who desire to go there'. [6]

Instead, it appeared that the new Government was reneging on this often repeated promise by continuing to impose restrictions on immigration and suggesting that the country be partitioned. Most of the blame was placed on the shoulders of Ernest Bevin as Secretary of State for Foreign Affairs. The editorial in the weekly, Zionist - affiliated *Palestine Post* of 2 September 1947, for example, commented that 'Mr Bevin still insists on treating Palestine as his private back-yard, into which the Jews want to intrude to annoy him'. [7] However, as Alan Bullock is at pains to emphasise in his acclaimed biography, Bevin did not start in office 'with a clean slate but stepped into a highly charged world situation' and 'nowhere was this more clearly and tragically illustrated than in the case of Palestine'. [8]

AC2 John Watson was transferred to Palestine in October 1946, travelling by road from his previous four month posting in Cairo, through Ismalia in the Suez Canal zone and the Sinai and Negev deserts to Jerusalem. At the time of his arrival, several Jewish insurgent groups were active in Palestine. The largest organisation, the Haganah, had its origins in the protection of Jewish settlements in the 1930s and was under the control of the Jewish Agency (the body established under the terms of the Mandate to advise and co-operate with the Palestine administration). An elite force known as the Palmach existed within the Haganah and operated as a full-time underground army. The Irgun Zvai Leumi were a yet more extreme force, becoming highly effective when Menachim Begin, later Prime Minister of Israel in the 1980s, took over as the group's Commander in 1943. The Haganah and the Irgun had markedly differing policies and tactics with regard to achieving independence:

> The Haganah's strategy envisaged a negotiated solution, in which constructive warfare was simply a pressure tactic and not the sole means of achieving the desired objective. The Irgun rejected a negotiated settlement; its aim was to achieve independence by inflicting a political/military defeat on Britain, forcing her to withdraw from the Mandate, and seizing power upon that withdrawal. Inevitably then, the Irgun's strategy required a higher level of violence and intensity of conflict. [9]

A third organisation, known as the Stern Gang or Lohamei Heruth Israel, was also known for its extreme tactics. Despite the disparities in approach the Jewish terrorist groups adopted a policy of 'united resistance' in the immediate post-war period. This co-operation ended when Irgun forces bombed the Secretariat of the

People run for cover as the King David Hotel, Jerusalem, the headquarters of the Secretariat of the Palestine Government, is blown up by Irgun terrorists on 22 July 1946. E 31973

Palestine Government, the King David Hotel, Jerusalem, on 22 July 1946. The action resulted in ninety-one casualties and caused the Haganah to retreat from extremist violence. The Irgun and the Stern Gang, however, increased their terrorist activities.

Although Watson arrived only three months after the infamous attack on the King David Hotel, his first letters from Palestine show little knowledge of, or interest in, the troubles. His only reference was to write in November, 'thank goodness the curfew was lifted last night, so the shops will be open in the evenings now, and the people in the curfew area not so surly'. [10] Rather, the accounts of his first few months are largely concerned with his training as an announcer with the Forces Broadcasting Service (FBS), which occupied the St Pierre convent in Jerusalem and had views of 'the Arab quarter, ... the Vale of Hebron, over the hills towards Jordan and the Dead Sea; and on the other side to the Citadel and the Old City'. The unit he served with was staffed by Army, RAF, Auxiliary Territorial Service (ATS), Women's Auxiliary Air Force personnel and a small number of (mainly Jewish) civilians. Their role was to entertain troops based in southern Palestine:

> From a modern studio on the summit of olive garbed Zion, just without the Old City walls, Elgar and Ellington, plays and poetry radiate through space for the entertainment of the British forces in the Middle East. One programme, transmitted on short wave reaches a regular circle of listeners as far afield as the Baltic, the Balkans and beyond Burma. [11]

In general, they were good days for Watson and he ends the letter written to his family on Christmas Day 1946 with the ebullient statement 'this is such an interesting job - I feel so happy with life now. Jerusalem is Jerusalem, and the Bethlehem service last night was simply wonderful!'.

In early 1947, the British Government decided to evacuate British service and civilian families from Palestine. In addition, security measures were tightened, with British troops moved into encampments behind barbed wire. As noted in the history of Forces Broadcasting, *The Microphone and the Frequency*, the personnel based in Jerusalem were averse to this new ruling and 'many managed to squeeze into cramped quarters on the top floor of St Pierre, outside the cantonment, while the former manager and Chief of the Jerusalem NAAFI were installed in the basement canteen to provide an ample but unhealthy diet'.[12] Although the authorities felt it necessary to introduce these new drastic measures in order to contain the terrorism, in a letter of 9 January Watson commented 'nothing ever happens to affect us, except the cafés are forbidden and guns must be carried when in uniform, and occasionally a noise which may have been a firework in the next door garden goes off miles away, doing little damage.' He was more concerned about the privations suffered by his parents and two sisters at home in England during the fuel crisis and bitter winter of 1946/47.

Arab and Jewish groups rejected British proposals for the division of Palestine into separate zones, administered as trusteeship territory, on 7 February. As a result the British Government referred the Palestine question to the United Nations Organisation and in May the UNO formed a Special Committee on Palestine (UNSCOP), composed of representatives from eleven states, which was required to report by 1 September.

John Watson was transferred from Jerusalem to No 4 Forces Broadcasting Unit, based on Mount Carmel, Haifa in February 1947. The station was housed in a former RAF meteorological station and its staff of twelve broadcast to the troops in northern Palestine, the Levant and Cyprus. Watson wrote home on 11 February to say he was relieved to be away from the cramped conditions of the St Pierre convent where forty people shared a small area. He had not escaped the petty restrictions though, and commented on the irony that only the terrorists had freedom of movement:

First we aren't allowed in town in 'civvies' (the *safest* way, of course)- then all the best part of the town is out of bounds, we have to go

about in fours - armed - even in these areas; the civilians and terrorists do as they please, the only people inconvenienced are us! That is just typical, of course, and no fewer people are blown up - the point is there is no use trying to stop the whole Zionist movement with petty orders, bans and curfews etc., which merely weaken the morale of British forces. To put it bluntly the troops don't see why the terrorists can go to the cinema fearlessly, whereas they (the soldiers) would have 14 days C.B. [confinement to barracks] for so doing, if caught. [13]

He thought, however, that these problems were not directly the fault of the Labour Government. It was 'no more Labour than Conservatives to blame really - [more] the cumulative effect of 25 years of "clueless" ruling and "addled administration".' [14]

In Haifa, Watson was well-placed to observe the arrival of the numerous refugee ships and the enforcement of the official policy, introduced in August 1946, of transporting the illegal immigrants to internment camps in Cyprus. In late February he had planned to attend a piano recital in the town, but:

At 2.30, when it should have started, they put postponed ... all over the posters - because a Jewish immigrant ship was coming in - all the shops had closed too. ...still we had a view of the destroyers all waiting for the ship, and crowds of people on their rooftops waiting; I tried to put myself in the position of one of

As a prevention against typhus a young Jewish boy is sprayed with DDT on 15 August 1946 before boarding a British troopship which was carrying illegal immigrants to a detention camp in Cyprus. E 32001

these poor people on the ship probably having suffered years of concentration camps ... All the people here are waiting to receive them, you can't help feeling sorry for them.

In early April he also wrote of the 'dreadful waste of oil' which had been caused by saboteurs from the militant terrorist group, the Lechi, attacking the Shell Oil Company refineries at Haifa in retaliation for the enforced trans-shipment of 1,500 illegal immigrants. [15]

The Mount Carmel studio was patrolled by a group of young Jewish guards and a friendship developed between Watson and one of them which would strongly influence his feeling about the British presence in Palestine and the refugee problem. They were almost the same age ('he is only 8 months older than me and does his eight hours guards a day, and yet manages to attend special school classes, as he is working for an engineer's course') and shared a love of classical music. During late shifts when John relayed BBC programmes or broadcast dance music, they passed the time by chatting. 'He does his "guarding" and I my "announcing".' On 25 April he wrote a long account describing the young refugee's experiences since the Second World War:

[He is] well educated, speaking English and French both quite well, also Hebrew - he is a Romanian born Jew, and was deported by the Germans in 1942 to a camp in Serbia, where he was all through the war till 1945; then he was freed, he and his friend found neither had a single member of their family alive - the Germans had killed or starved them all - so they set out on a "legal" immigrant ship, with others in a like plight - that was in July-August 1945. Now he has been in Palestine for nearly two years ...

It seems dreadful to think of so many people whose fate has been like his or worse, having to come over in those filthy overcrowded illegal ships (there's one off the coast just now I believe), and then get turned out to grass in concentration camps in Cyprus, for ages, simply because only about 1,000 legal immigrants come in a year straight from Europe; the others have all been through the immigrant ships and Cyprus camps. Seeing how the troops treat ordinary civilians ... I hate to think how they treat them in the camps.

The refugee ship *Exodus* reaches Haifa in July 1947 crammed with Jewish refugees. (Reproduced by kind permission of the Britain / Israel Public Affairs Centre.) HU 63093

Two refugees from the *Exodus* at Haifa in July 1947. (Reproduced with the kind permission of BIPAC.) HU 63094

In the summer of 1947 Watson wrote home describing a sailing trip undertaken with a family friend, Major Philip Keymer, who was also serving in Palestine.

... cruising around before the start [of the race] we saw the part of the harbour given over to the derelict immigrant ships ... and among them the latest arrival - the *Exodus 1947* ... How it got across the Red [Sea] (far less the Atlantic!) I can't imagine. Think of one of those large river steamers - like floating hotels, all superstructure, and little hull. Then imagine its primitive ancestor back in the days when steam was just beginning to challenge sail, and you'll picture the 4,500 inhabited horror ship. [16]

The *Exodus 1947* was a converted ferry, purchased with American funds, which had left Port de Bouc, west of Marseilles, crowded with 4,493 Jewish passengers which the organisers deliberately planned to land in Palestine while members of the United Nations Special Committee were present in the region collecting information for their report. Royal Naval personnel boarded the boat off Palestine in the early hours of 18 July and a fight for control went on for hours. British vessels then took the *Exodus 1947* into port where the forced transfer of the immigrants into three British ships was witnessed by members of the UN Committee and by a large number of journalists.

Rather than being sent to Cyprus, the refugees were shipped back to France where the authorities refused to force them to land. The British Cabinet then decided to send them on to Hamburg, in the zone of Germany which was controlled by British forces. In the words of Nicholas Bethell:

> It seemed like an act of calculated inhumanity to send Jewish survivors of concentration camps back to the country where these horrors had been perpetrated and where their relatives had died. Far from 'making an example' of the *Exodus* and rallying the world against the organisers of illegal immigration, Bevin succeeded only in shocking the world community into deeper sympathy for the Zionist enterprise. [17]

John Watson wrote that the *Exodus* affair was 'a gross political bloomer' [18] and the return of the Jews to Hamburg 'so unforgivable that I cannot fathom out what it means. I feel sure that the people at home in England can't have wanted it, at whatever cost to Bevin's loss of face'. [19] He also endorsed the sentiments expressed in a *Palestine Post* editorial and enclosed the cutting for his family to read:

> The refugees of the *Exodus 1947* have become symbolic of the whole Jewish race in dispersion, or to use the word now fashionable, in displacement. Their return to Germany is a hideous confirmation of their displacement and is in fact and principle diametrically against the findings of the United Nations Committee and of humanitarian opinion the world over.

In the summer of 1947, the number of clashes between British forces and the various Jewish terrorist groups escalated; each terrorist outrage led to reprisals from the British forces and then another act of brutality from the Jews. On 6 August, Watson wrote to his family describing this cycle of retaliatory violence. Three members of the Irgun 'all young boys, were caught while assisting a jail break, in which no-one was killed. They have a so-called "trial" and are sentenced to be hanged, by the military laws of an occupying foreign army'. This in turn led to the kidnapping and assassination in Nathanya of two British non-commissioned officers, Clifford Martin and Mervyn Paice. Their bodies were found booby-trapped and hanged and the incident showed according to one historian 'the absolute alienation of government from community' where 'troops were subject not only to incessant harrying to which ... they could produce no really effective military response, but as the struggle darkened into the semblance of blood feud, to kidnapping, flogging and execution'. [20] Watson, however, was less willing to justify the reprisals in this manner, describing the ensuing actions carried out by troops and police:

> The next day a Palestine Police (British) armoured car-load of avenging (British) angels let loose hell into a bus load of ordinary Jewish civilians in the middle of Tel Aviv. 5 innocent people (including an eight year old girl) died and 70 were seriously injured in this outrage. Yet that is considered only natural, and of course hushed up by the authorities. Do you remember those films about the Nazis in occupied Europe, when you saw German cars sweeping through towns, mowing down the crowds with machine-gun fire? [21]

In the letter written home in the following week, he described the turmoil and disruption which followed:

> There are days, weeks, sometimes months of six or seven o'clock curfews ... people shot unwarned if merely seen behind unshuttered windows ... soldiers dissatisfied with conditions and trigger happy, firing at the slightest opportunity. ... A man looks out of a window, a soldier fires 'over his head' and hits

TEL-AVIV SHOTS: FIVE JEWS KILLED, MANY INJURED　　*ATTLEE MAY TELL OF CUTS IN BREAD AND BUTTER*　　*HOLIDAYS ABROAD BARRED FOR BRITISH CHILDREN*

HANGED BRITONS: Picture that will shock the world

Food from abroad is cut

BUTTER RATION MAY BE HALVED

By GUY EDEN

MR. ATTLEE, in his speech to the Commons next Wednesday in the two-day state-of-the-nation debate, is expected to announce these cuts in the drive to save dollars:

BUTTER ration down by a half—it now represents a weekly average of 3ozs.

BREAD allowance down by a quarter—to an average of 27 BUs a month; and

PETROL ration down by a third — the basic unit to revert to the one-gallon value instead of being worth 1½ gallons as now.

MEAT is also likely to be cut from today's 1s. 2d. worth a week (2d. worth in corned beef). The cut will not be severe at first, but the ration may have to be reduced again later.

SUGAR is also believed to be on the Premier's cut-it-down list.

But the MARGARINE ration—usually average at present, is less—may be slightly increased.

Food from our land is wasted

Cabbages fed to sheep

By KENNETH PIPE

FARMERS in the West Country, dealing with a better-than-expected early harvest, are finding markets glutted with vegetables.

Many have stopped digging potatoes because Bristol and other towns are over-supplied with "earlies" at about 11d. a lb. Unless arrangements can be made for switching the potatoes to other parts of the country, the farmers say they will lose heavily.

Cabbages (2d. to 4d. a lb. in the shops and cauliflowers (4d. to 5d. a lb.) are also piling up. Some farmers have turned sheep on to cabbage fields rather than suffer losses on the market.

Lettuces (tempting the housewife from 1d. to 5d. each) are being dumped at 1d. each by retailers.

Runner beans were sold in Evesham (Worcs.) wholesale market yesterday at 1s. for a glut, not but there was no bid for peas. The beans sold at 4d. a lb. in local shops.

Food in Argentina is rotting

Senor Miranda burns the oil

BUENOS AIRES, Thursday.

Shots in Tel-Aviv: 5 Jews die

STAY-PUT SHIPS FOR CYPRUS?

Express Political Correspondent

THE Cabinet is considering several other landing places for the 4,500 Jewish illegal immigrants off the French coast if it proves impossible to land them in France.

A "tropical island" is one

From PETER DUFFIELD: Jerusalem, Thursday

FIVE Jews were killed and several wounded tonight in a clash in the all-Jewish city of Tel-Aviv, twelve hours after the finding of two British sergeants hanged by Irgun thugs in a sweet eucalyptus grove.

The police, in an official statement, blamed

IN A GROVE OF EUCALYPTUS...

RADIOED from Jerusalem last night, this Daily Express picture was taken in a eucalyptus grove south of Nathanya, Palestine.

The bodies of murdered Clifford Martin and Mervyn Paice—British security sergeants—hang from saplings.

The hands of both victims are bound behind their backs. Pieces of shirt have been wrapped round their heads. To one body is pinned a notice: "This is the sentence of Irgun's High Tribunal."

A booby-trap explosion threw the photographer to the ground after this picture was taken. The film was salvaged from his smashed camera.

— Wanted for

999 AT MIDNIGHT

Woman held

Express Staff Reporter

THE burglar alarm started to ring at 12.15 this morning in a gown shop in Old Brompton-road, S.W.

It often does. Every time it goes off one of the neighbours dials 999.

This morning it was a doctor who ran to the phone.

Police found panes of glass smashed in the shop which had been entered by forcing D. B. Stannock.

People at the flats above leaned out of bedroom windows and saw them climb a wall down a drain

ABBEY WEDDING FOR THE PRINCESS

On November 20

Express Staff Reporter

PRINCESS ELIZABETH and Lieutenant Philip Mountbatten will be married at Westminster Abbey at 11.30 a.m. on Thursday, November 20. It was announced from Buckingham Palace last night.

The King had revealed this at a Privy Council meeting earlier in the day when he gave formal consent to the marriage.

Preliminary arrangements will be made before the end of next week when the Royal Family start their holiday at Balmoral. The holiday may be cut to enable the Princess to be in London for first fittings at her dressmakers.

DRIVE IN STATE

It is expected that Dr. Fisher, Archbishop of Canterbury, assisted by the Dean of Westminster, Dr. Alan C. Don, will solemnise the marriage, with Dr. Garbett, Archbishop of York, taking part in the service.

There will almost certainly be a state drive from Buckingham Palace to the Abbey.

Arrangements have been made to allow all the Princess's wedding gifts in the state rooms of St. James's Palace. The public will be admitted on payment of a sum which will be given to a charity.

It will probably be an austerity wedding—morning clothes for men and long dresses for women taking the place of Court dress.

'Tell Dutch to go back'

NEW YORK, Thursday.—The war in Java should be called off at once and the Dutch should go back to their original positions, India's spokesman, Mr. B. R. Sen, told the Security Council today.

Otherwise the Dutch would have an unfairly favourable advantage when the time came for talks.

The Dutch representative Dr. Van Kleffen said his Government was going to invite other Governments to send delegates to Indonesia to report their findings.

Dutch warship sunk

BATAVIA, Thursday.—The Dutch admitted today that Indonesians have sunk a Dutch warship off Central Java. The city of Malang has been captured from the Indonesians.—Express News Service.

'Undeclared war'

NEW YORK, Thursday.—Greece tonight charged Albania, Bulgaria and Yugoslavia with waging undeclared war against her and demanded action by the Security Council.—Reuter.

Baby, 1½ lb.

A baby weighing one and a half pounds at birth has lived at Queen Charlotte's Hospital, London, S.E.

BACK THEY G

The front page of the *Daily Express* of 1 August 1947 carrying the story of the two British sergeants whose booby-trapped bodies were discovered in Nathanya. (Reproduced by kind permission of the British Library, Newspaper Library.) HU 63101

a woman in the eye (in a flat above behind curtained windows) - she is blind now and her face horribly mutilated. All of this probably never reaches the London pressmen, because they don't want to hear it. [22]

This was a correct assumption - in the summer of 1947 British newspapers were reporting with outrage the execution of the two British sergeants in Palestine. *The Times*, for example, wrote on 1 August that the men 'were kidnapped unarmed and defenceless. They were murdered for no offence. As a last indignity their bodies were employed to lure into a minefield the comrades who sought to give them a Christian burial'. [23] And the *Observer* held that 'the mimicry of Nazi methods by the terrorists leads straight to the conclusion that we cannot go on sending our young soldiers to the odious cauldron of crime and passion'. [24] In August, Watson wrote to ask:

> Do people say at home, 'The only thing to do about the Jews is to have them shot "en masse". The Germans were quite right of course, I suppose we can be thankful they wiped out as many Jews as they did'? My only reaction to these remarks (which are usually not meant as jokes, and are pretty universal) is to feel like getting a Bren gun in the mess of the typically clottish British uncultured soldiers.

In fact, the news of the sergeants' deaths did have a dramatic effect on British public opinion which 'became increasingly disgusted with the whole affair and anxious to be rid of the burden of responsibility'. [25] There were anti-Jewish riots in Liverpool, Manchester, Glasgow and London, and synagogues and Jewish-owned shops were attacked.

Watson shared the view that it was time for the British to withdraw from Palestine, but his view was based on an abhorrence of colonialism rather than sympathy with the plight of the British peace-keeping troops. On 7 September he wrote that 'the sooner we accept we have grossly mismanaged the Mandate, acknowledged defeat over the Palestine problem generally and decided to clear out of the country ... - the better'. Undoubtedly his impression of the situation in Palestine was coloured by the nature of his duties. His experience as an announcer with the Forces Broadcasting Units in Jerusalem and Haifa clearly differed from that of other members of the British forces, whose time was spent controlling riots, carrying out cordon and search operations, invigilating curfews and guarding important areas such as telephone exchanges and military installations. Although the terrorism came to affect him far more directly before his departure from Palestine, his major hardship at this time was the sense of claustrophobia which prevailed as the British troops were forced to spend an increasing amount of time in their barracks. Writing to his family in September 1947, he commented 'there is absolutely no news from this concentration camp! ... what maddens me most is not being able to go out for walks alone, or in pairs - FOUR

are needed to go anywhere on foot - two in a truck in daytime. It's driving us almost mad and the result is a lot of friction in this small camp of 15 people'. Yet as ever he was keen to point out that the situation was worse for the Jewish and Arab communities:

> How nice it must be to go out alone in civilian clothes ... For the last six months, that has been an offence punishable by sentence without trial to some awful punishment ... and yet it is the obvious negation of freedom. When this is suffered by an army of occupation in a country which this army has no right to be in, then what of the civilians - their life is equally hard - premises shut down at short notice, and people evicted from their homes without warning, all without trial or right to appeal.

For Watson and his colleagues, the only relief from this increasingly oppressive atmosphere came with the occasional spells of leave taken on the Lebanese border at Ras-el-Nikora. After a visit in September 1947 he wrote that he 'was transferred from the land of Strife and Restrictions to a land of paradise'. On the journey he saw neighbouring Jewish settlements and Arab villages where there were 'no signs of trouble'. It 'was just marvellous, no guns, no zones, no soldiers, and a real town at night.' He continued with the optimistic statement 'still we hope for peace - the last refugee ship was only a landing craft!!'

The United Nations Special Committee on Palestine produced their report in the summer of 1947 and it was signed at Geneva on 31 August. It recommended that 'the Mandate of Palestine should be terminated at the earliest practicable date'. [26] The majority plan opted for the partition of the country into separate Arab and Jewish states and for the city of Jerusalem to be placed under an international trusteeship. During the transitional period, the United Kingdom was to carry on the administration of Palestine and to admit a further 150,000 Jewish refugees.   On 4 December, the British Cabinet fixed the date for the Mandate to end as 15 May 1948, with the total military withdrawal to be completed by 1 August. Watson noted in a letter home that the Yishuv hung flags in the streets as a mark of their delight at this news. [27] As noted by Nicholas Bethell, 'the main battleground was no longer between the Jews and the British. The violent Arab protests that greeted the decision to set up a Jewish state escalated within a few days into a series of killings and counter-killings that would continue for decades'. [28] The British forces and the Palestine Police attempted to keep the peace between the Arabs and Jews, but the situation deteriorated in the final months 'until their activity was confined solely to maintaining their own security and making sure they would be able to depart as planned'. [29] Watson noted that Arab violence became more prevalent at this time and 'a party of them machine-gunned two Jewish buses, killing seven; but that is quite an ordinary occurrence these days ... Anything more cowardly I can't imagine than lying in wait for, and machine-gunning, a crowded bus'.

In December, John Watson transferred from Haifa back to Jerusalem, and as 1947 slipped into 1948 saw the clashes between the Jewish and Arab communities intensify. On New Year's Eve 1947, Watson wrote that the previous week had 'gone by in a whirl' and 'the "troubles" (using the Irish expression of understatement) get more every day, and the English less involved every day':

> The worst so far was in Haifa yesterday, when a group of Arabs going to work at an English refinery were hit by a bomb thrown by IZLs [Irgun terrorists] in a car. 7 were killed, and the rest went into their workplace and set on the local Jewish employees there, with daggers and guns and hands, and killed 41 in cold blood! That's how one act starts another. Yesterday afternoon we watched a Jewish convoyed funeral held up by Arabs in an Arab village, where a pitched battle occurred before the procession got through the Mt. of Olives Cemetery (we have a tremendous view from the roof here - over the east side of Jerusalem). Then the Arabs ambushed a bus load of nurses, and shot them up, wounding and killing several. As a reprisal Jews threw a bomb at a market crowd in Damascus Gate, killing seven. And so it goes on. The Palestine Police act very bravely to stop it, and the troops are kept away from any trouble there is. It is obvious the Government is not interfering, apart from sacrificing the inadequate Police Force.

Part of the strain of these months for Watson and his colleagues was the sheer hard work caused by staff shortages as long-standing members of the FBS were demobilised. Writing to his sister Anne in October 1947, he admitted that 'for once your lazy brother was really working morning, noon and night - always straining to

sound pleasant to his adoring public.' For the previous few days he had spent 27 out of 52 hours on air and for every two or three hours actually broadcasting it was necessary to spend at least an hour rehearsing and scripting a programme. His workload increased when the two civilian Jewish broadcasters, Esther Lendner and Ziona Caspi, were forced to leave because of worries that they would be attacked during their journeys to and from work. In Watson's words the only consolation was that radio was almost 'the only form of entertainment left now to the troops sealed up in the thousand and one camps all over the country.'

At the end of 1947, both the electricity and telephone lines between the FBS Headquarters at St Pierre in Jerusalem and the associated transmitting station twelve miles away at Beit Jala were cut. The only way for transmissions to continue was for Watson to base himself at the transmitting station. From Beit Jala he wrote:

> The reason we're here is that the Jews have cut the 'phone and other ground lines between here and town, and the Arabs won't repair them, this being an Arab part of the countryside. We are thus not only cut off from Jerusalem by phone or line but also almost by road. The Arabs are trying to stop the army from getting through to Hebron, to help the Jewish settlements attacked by Arab masses. The RAF "Spits" are over all day preparing to strafe the Arabs if necessary, and the latter building walls across the roads. But our trucks have got through to Jerusalem so far OK - if only once a day to get the records and programmes we put over. [30]

Broadcasting in these conditions was no mean feat, as on arrival Watson 'found only a little desk with 2 turntables, a "mike" and 2 BBC receiving sets tuned in, all in a draughty corridor in a hut, which was otherwise a kind of toolshed store'.

On 21 January 1948, Watson to wrote to his family with 'mixed good and bad news from this end' and reported that his rifle had been stolen from his room at the end of the previous week. At the time he and the other military personnel resident in the building were in the NAAFI watching the weekly film show. Strictly speaking, Watson should have taken the rifle with him at all times, but it was usual practice to secure firearms to the beds in their dormitory when personnel were in the building and carry them at all other times. The loss of weapons was not an uncommon occurrence and Watson observed that it was the tenth to be stolen from their accommodation in a short period, with four Arab guards mysteriously disappearing at the same time! 'The authorities admit the Arab Legion is no longer a "trustworthy force"', he commented, 'and that we must "expect losses" but refuse to give us better protection, and help when the arms go. A farcical situation.'

Watson and others spent the night searching neighbouring Arab villages for the rifle but to no avail. The RAF police questioned him the next morning and 'instead of putting me under open arrest they advised me nicely not to be seen out of St Pierre grounds'. A report on the case was to be presented to the Commanding Officer of AHQ Levant and the RAF police estimated a sentence of seven to fourteen days, with the possibility of 'Confinement to Barracks' because Watson was vital to the short-staffed unit. He ends his letter by saying that at first he 'had visions of 6 months penal servitude in a "glass house" in the desert somewhere' but had now resolved that 'there's nothing to worry about. I wouldn't have told you anything until it was all over if I had thought it was going to be bad.'

The question of his punishment was overshadowed in the following correspondence by the news that the Chief Engineer at the St Pierre studio, Sergeant Patrick 'Dixie' Dean, had been killed in a terrorist incident near the Jaffa Gate. John and Dixie had been good friends and in May 1947 spent a period of leave together in Cyprus:

> ... it is an awful shock to us all, and [I] really don't know how to put it. A couple of our trucks were coming back from the cinema in the zone, where all British Forces go in the evening, and the Arabs at a barrier near the Jaffa Gate opened up on them at 40 yards range. My great friend Dixie Dean was shot and died instantaneously with a bullet through the heart, two others are recovering from severe wounds in hospital, and two others were released the next morning after treatment. It was a miracle that the others (there were about 12 in all) were alright.

> I was not even on the trucks - luckily so it is easier for me to talk of it dispassionately - it seems so quite unreal that Dixie's no longer here. The Palestine Police came to their rescue, and the Arabs fled into their homes - but I think will not be arrested. The official

excuse is that they took us for a Police Convoy of food to relieve the Jewish quarter of the Old City. But that is a poor excuse and doesn't really mean too much. [31]

He reassured his family by writing that he was too busy to dwell on this and that the staff of the Forces Broadcasting Unit were 'quite safe and unmolested behind our walls, and no-one really wants to do anything about us, as we provide the only entertainment, these days, for miles around.'

There are in fact few letters beyond this date. Between 17 February and 14 March 1948, Watson was tried for the loss of his rifle and spent two to three weeks in a Royal Air Force prison. Another broadcaster stationed at Jerusalem at this time, Staff Sergeant Arthur Appleton, recalls that the RAF police came for Watson when he was on air presenting his classical concert programme. Appleton 'pleaded with them to let him finish' but the police would not wait. Johnny Watson left between records and two RAF policemen, with another announcer squeezing in as the detention party led him out'. [32] Despite Watson's hopes for a lenient sentence, it seems that he was harshly treated in prison and left the RAF bitter and disillusioned with military life. [33] His long-awaited demobilisation order came through in March 1948 and he wrote:

> Well I won't bore you with the sordid details ... all I need to say here is that it has left me with a perpetual hatred of the injustice of military law and injustice generally of justice if you see what I mean. And that not so much for myself luckily in the RAF, but for those army lads doing 6 month sentences for the same "offence".

> Still I haven't yet lost complete faith in mankind really - so all could be a lot worse; and I certainly appreciate being able to walk once again in freedom, and eat enough to fill me! [34]

His final letter from the Middle East was sent from Forces Broadcasting, Kabrit, Egypt and said 'when you open this (I really think as well as hope) your long-lost creature should at last be actually in England...' [35]

Without his period of national service in the Middle East, John would have made an uninterrupted transition from public school to Oxford. Instead he was

Members of the Irgun parading in triumph through Tel Aviv in May 1948 to celebrate the creation of the state of Israel. (From the Fred Csasznik collection) HU 54635

to encounter a wide range of experiences and people - in terms of nationality, class and religion. His exposure to Palestine at the height of the disturbances was undoubtedly intense and formative, and his training with the Forces Broadcasting Service was to form the basis for his career in journalism and radio. In 1951, after completing a two year degree in Politics, Philosophy and Economics at Trinity College he moved to France and worked for French Radio's English Service and then on the English desk of Agence France-Presse. In the 1960s, he returned to England and joined the BBC World Service where he worked until retirement. His obituary in the BBC in-house magazine *Ariel* describes him as 'a much admired chief sub-editor ... turning down opportunities for promotion with a repeated "I'm quite happy with what I'm doing".' [36] He died suddenly in November 1990.

The British withdrawal from Palestine in 1948 marked the end of another chapter of the troubled history of the Middle East. On 14 May, Britain relinquished the mandate and the Jewish National Provincial Council proclaimed the State of Israel. Fighting broke out immediately between the Jewish and Arab factions. By this time, Watson had ended his two and half year national service and had been back in England for two months. His well-expressed and thought-provoking letters offer a valuable insight into these troubled times. At the height of the furore over the execution by the Irgun of the two intelligence sergeants, there can have been few British troops who would have sent home an article by the writer Arthur Koestler which explained the violence from the Jewish standpoint. The piece, which John Watson described in a letter to his mother as a 'really clear piece of thinking you should take to heart', included the following explanation of the terrorists' motivation:

Every morning when you open your paper you feel sick with fear that your boy might have been kidnapped or blown to pieces by Jewish terrorists. I am a person who sympathises with the terrorists and ... I am writing to you to explain these circumstances.

I am not speaking lightly of terror; during several years I have lived in the same anxiety, for persons near to me, which you feel for your son. The persons were my mother and her family; the danger which threatened them, as Jews in German-controlled territory, was death by poison gas or quicklime. My mother was the only one who escaped. Her sister, her sister's daughter and two grandchildren were gassed. My mother's brother committed suicide. Every single Jewish terrorist in Palestine has a similar story. This is the first fact you have to let sink in; without this background you will understand nothing. [37]

Watson did not forget the extent of Jewish suffering during the Holocaust and sympathised with the Jewish desire to set up a homeland in the Middle East. His accounts also show an impressive understanding of the wider context of international affairs which influenced British policy in this region. Perhaps, however, the most notable theme is that for twenty year old Watson the British Empire was no longer a positive force.

Notes

1. Michael Carver, *War Since 1945*, Weidenfeld & Nicholson, London, 1980, p 3.

2. The historian Alan Bullock points out that during Ernest Bevin's time as Foreign Secretary 'the framework of international relations was entirely re-made'. The issues Bevin faced included the first phase of the Cold War, the Marshall Plan, the North Atlantic Alliance, the division of Germany and the independence of India and Pakistan. See Alan Bullock, *Ernest Bevin, Foreign Secretary 1945-1951*, Oxford University Press, Oxford, 1985, p xiv.

3. From 'Report of the Palestine Committee', 8/9/45, CP(45) 156, as quoted in Bullock, op cit, p 70.

4. As expressed by Theodore Herzl at the first Zionist Congress in Basle, 1897 and quoted in G Rowley, *Israel into Palestine*, Mansell Publishing, 1984, p 17.

5. Department of Documents, Papers of Rex Keating. *Middle East Opinion* 20/1/47, p 3 from an article reprinted from *Harpers*.

6. Department of Documents, Papers of John Wells Watson. From an article written by Arthur Koestler for the *New Statesman* which was re-published in the *Palestine Post* and sent by Watson to his mother on 1/9/47.

7. *Palestine Post*, 2/9/47, Watson Papers.

8. Bullock, op cit, p 44.

9. D A Charters, *The British Army and Jewish Insurgency in Palestine, 1945-47*, Macmillan, London, p 48.

10. Watson Papers, letter from Watson to family, 8/11/46.

11. S Maxton writing in *Parade* on 29/11/47, held in the Watson Papers.

12. Doreen Taylor, *The Microphone and the Frequency: Forty Years of Forces Broadcasting*, Heinemann, London, 1983, p 72.

13. Watson Papers, Watson to his sister Anne, l0/3/47.

14. John Watson was being uncharacteristically generous to the post-war Labour administration here. Many of his comments on the Government were less favourable. On 30/4/47, for example, he wrote 'if March [1948] doesn't see me out [demobilised], I think some of us will come over to England as stowaways, and shoot Bevin, Shinwell, Stafford Cripps and whoever else is responsible for the regrettable state of affairs. I'm really rather surprised to hear that no-one else thought of that during the winter Labour bungles'.

15. D Taylor, op cit, p 68.

16. Watson Papers, letter from Watson to family, 28/7/47.

17. Nicholas Bethell, *The Palestine Triangle*, André Deutsch, London, 1979, p 343.

18. Watson Papers, letter from Watson to family, 2/9/47.

19. Watson Papers, letter from Watson to family, 15/9/47.

20. Charles Townshend, *Britain's Civil Wars: Counter-insurgency in the Twentieth Century*, Faber & Faber, London, 1986, p 115.

21. Watson Papers, letter from Watson to family, 6/8/47.

22. Watson Papers, letter from Watson to family, 15/9/47.

23. Quoted in Bethell, op cit, p 338.

24. George Lichtheim, 'The British Press and Palestine' in *The Palestine Post*, August 1947.

25. M Carver, op cit, p 10.

26. 'United Nations Special Committee on Palestine 1947 - Summary of Recommendations', Government of Palestine, p 1.

27. Watson Papers, letter from Watson to family, 1/12/47.

28. N Bethell, op cit, p 351.

29. M Carver, op cit, p ll.

30. Watson Papers, letter from Watson to family, 15/1/48.

31. Watson Papers, letter from Watson to family, 2/2/48.

32. D Taylor, op cit, p 69.

33. Anne Christopherson (Watson's sister) to author.

34. Watson Papers, letter from Watson to Anne, 15/3/48.

35. Watson Papers, letter from Watson to family, 4/4/48.

36. Dennis Benton writing in *Ariel*, December 1990.

37. Arthur Koestler, as above.

Further Reading

David Dilks, 'The British View of Security: Europe and a Wider World, 1945-48' in Olav Riste [ed], *Western Security: The Formative Years*, Norwegian University Press, Norway.
Sir William Jackson, *Withdrawal from Empire: A Military View*, Batsford Ltd, London, 1986.
W R Lewis and Stookey (eds), *The End of the Palestine Mandate*, I B Tauris.
Gwyn Rowley, *Israel into Palestine*, Mansell Publishing, London, 1984.
Doreen Taylor, *A Microphone and a Frequency: Forty Years of Forces Broadcasting*, Heinemann, London, 1983.
Charles Townshend, *Britain's Civil Wars: Counter-insurgency in the Twentieth Century*, Faber & Faber, London, 1986.
Major R D Wilson, *Cordon and Search: With 6th Airborne Division in Palestine*, Gale and Polden, Aldershot, 1949.

Acknowledgements

Special thanks to Mrs Anne Christopherson, John Watson's sister, who kindly donated the collection and provided additional information; to Alan Grace, Head of Broadcasting at the Services Sound and Vision Corporation and former member of the Forces Broadcasting Service; and to Mandie Lieberman of the Britain / Israel Public Affairs Centre for help with picture research.

The British Pacific Fleet of 1944-45, and its newspaper, *Pacific Post*

Colin Bruce and Terry Charman

Colin Bruce and Terry Charman are research assistants in the Department of Printed Books.

The grandly-named British Pacific Fleet was brought into existence on 22 November 1944, when Admiral Sir Bruce Fraser's Eastern Fleet at Trincomalee was split into two new forces.

The more modern ships, including all the fleet carriers and the new battleships *King George V* and *Howe*, went with Fraser as the core of a powerful, hard-hitting force to fight alongside the Americans in the Pacific. The rump became the British East Indies Fleet, to which fell the less glamorous task of maintaining British control of the Indian Ocean and assisting the army in its liberation of Burma. [1]

The creation of the British Pacific Fleet (BPF) marked the return of the Royal Navy to a theatre from which it had been ingloriously hounded in 1942. Since then, however, the back of the Imperial Japanese Navy had been broken at Coral Sea, Midway and the Great Marianas Turkey Shoot, and the enemy had been forced onto the strategic defensive.

Admiral Ernest King, Commander-in-Chief of the navy which had inflicted these defeats, had little enthusiasm for the belated return of the British. To King, the BPF would be a useless encumbrance and a drain on the extraordinary logistical system he had built up to sustain his ships in the vastness of the Pacific. He was forced to accept a British presence only after Churchill had put the matter directly to President Roosevelt during their Quebec conference, and only on the understanding the BPF should be self-supporting. In other words, it must bring with it sufficient tankers, supply and repair ships to maintain itself without adding to the US Navy's logistical burden. [2]

Having established the BPF in the teeth of such opposition, Churchill and the British Chiefs of Staff remained painfully aware that King might attempt to relegate their ships to side-show operations while the Americans fought out the decisive battles alone. They therefore pressed for the BPF to be deployed as part of Admiral Chester Nimitz's island-hopping thrust across the Central Pacific - the drive which would lead most directly to the Japanese home islands.

At the same time the senior appointments for the new fleet were finalised. The Commander-in-Chief, BPF would be Admiral Sir Bruce Fraser, the popular 57-year-old who, as C-in-C Home Fleet, had caught and sunk the *Scharnhorst* off the North Cape. The officer chosen to be Fraser's deputy, and to exercise tactical control of the fleet, was a 56-year-old Cornishman, Vice-Admiral Sir

Bernard Rawlings. Although largely forgotten today, Rawlings had made a name for himself as a cruiser admiral in the Mediterranean, where he had been wounded during the Battle of Crete. He was also no stranger to the Far East, having served as British naval attaché in Tokyo prior to the war. The fleet's carrier commander would be Rear Admiral Sir Philip Vian, the hero of the *Altmark* incident back in 1940, and more recently in charge of a carrier force during the invasion of Sicily. Five years younger than Rawlings, the ruthless and abrasive Vian was to prove a difficult subordinate, and the poor relations between the two were to be an additional headache for Fraser.

The other important sea going commands, of the 4th Cruiser Squadron, the BPF Destroyers and the Fleet Train, went to Rear Admirals Patrick Brind, John Edelsten and Douglas Fisher.

During a meeting with Nimitz and Admiral Ray Spruance (with whose US 5th Fleet Fraser hoped to operate) at Pearl Harbor in December 1944, Fraser was asked if the BPF could hit the oil refineries on Sumatra while in transit from Ceylon to Australia, and the suggestion was readily taken up. [3]

A preliminary strike by *Indomitable* and *Illustrious* on 20 December failed to find its main objective - the refinery at Pangkalan Brandan - because of bad weather, but a second by *Indomitable, Victorious* and *Indefatigable* on 4 January 1945 inflicted considerable damage on this, the most northerly of the lucrative oil targets on the island. Those further south were left, as Nimitz and Spruance had suggested, until after the fleet had left Trincomalee for the last time.

The fleet sailed for Australia on 16 January, with all four carriers flying off strikes against the Pladjoe and Soengei Gerong refineries on 24 and 29 January. The raids cost the fleet a number of aircraft, but were useful not only in cutting the output of the refineries but also in highlighting a few shortcomings in training - particularly as regards radio discipline and co-operation between the strike aircraft and their escorting fighters. Had the ships been able to remain on station a third strike might have finished off both targets, but shortage of fuel dictated that the fleet press on for Australia, where it put in at Fremantle on 4 February. [4]

After a fortnight enjoying the hospitality of Sydney, the fleet sailed for its staging base at Manus, in the Admiralty Islands, where it arrived on 7 March to carry out exercises. Fighting was at that time continuing in the Philippines, where Manila had just fallen to MacArthur's forces, and on Iwo Jima, where the Japanese garrison still clung to their bunkers in the eastern end of

The Pacific, 1944-45

the island. The decision about which of these two prongs of the American advance - MacArthur in the South West Pacific or Nimitz in the Central Pacific - the BPF should reinforce still lay with Admiral King. Not until 14 March did he finally confirm that Fraser's fleet would be joining Nimitz's command, as the British had wanted all along. Fraser's HQ in Sydney relayed the order to Rawlings at Manus, who brought the BPF forward to Ulithi to join the American ships assembling there for the invasion of Okinawa - the last stepping stone before the Japanese home islands themselves.

On 22 March Rawlings, flying his flag in the *King George V*, took the carriers *Indomitable, Victorious, Illustrious* and *Indefatigable*, the battleships *King George V* and *Howe*, the cruisers *Swiftsure, Gambia, Black Prince, Argonaut* and *Euryalus*, and eleven destroyers to sea as an operational task force of the US 5th Fleet. In reality the designation bestowed by the Americans, Task Force 57, considerably flattered the British, since on paper it placed it on a par with their own Task Force 58 - a force many times its size. [5]

After topping up with fuel from its own tankers, TF57 closed the islands of Miyako and Ishigaki to commence suppressive raids on the airfields there on 26 March. It then settled into the unfamiliar routine of sustained offensive operations at the end of a long supply line - two of three days of strikes, followed by a day or two to rendezvous with the tankers and supply ships and replenish stocks of aircraft, ordnance and fuel.

While the British carriers were out of the action, an American task group of four escort carriers took their places to keep up the pressure. [6]

On 1 April the Americans began their landings on Okinawa, exactly as planned. The same day TF57 had to fight off its first kamikaze attack, one plane breaking through the defending fighters to crash directly onto the carrier *Indefatigable* and another managing to bomb and cripple the destroyer *Ulster*. Though the *Ulster* had to be towed off to Leyte for repairs, the damaged carrier was back in action again less than an hour after the attack, her armoured flight deck having proved highly effective. (This was a feature shared by all the British carriers but omitted from American ones on the grounds that the added weight would have reduced their aircraft capacity.) The ship's American liaison officer was quoted as commenting ruefully 'when a kamikaze hits a US carrier, it's six months repair at Pearl. In a Limey carrier it's a case of "sweepers, man your brooms".' [7]

Illustrious was hit in the side by another kamikaze on 6 April and was withdrawn for an overdue refit when her sister ship *Formidable* arrived on 14 April, although most Japanese strength was directed at the American groups around Okinawa itself - the landing and support units and the carriers trying to shield them.

TF57's attentions were switched from Mikayo and Ishigaki to northern Formosa from 11 to 13 April, after which the force was scheduled to retire for major replenishment. Knowing that the American groups further north were being pounded, however, Rawlings twice extended his period on station - a small gesture which was nevertheless well received. [8] When TF57 finally broke off to put in at San Pedro Roads it had been continuously at sea for thirty-two days - the record for a British fleet since Nelson's day. [9]

They arrived back at Mikayo on 4 May and Rawlings, believing the kamikaze threat had diminished, decided to go close inshore and use his big guns against the enemy for the first time. Unfortunately, in detaching his two battleships, plus five cruisers and the destroyers needed to escort them, he left Vian's carriers in an exposed position. The threat had not receded, and the fleet's reduced firepower proved unable to cope. *Formidable* was left burning, and her aircraft had to land on the other carriers. [10] *Indomitable*, Vian's flagship, was damaged by blast. Reunited with the bombardment force, the carriers limped off to the south east to lick their wounds. *Formidable*'s fires were extinguished and the ship made ready again by nightfall, providing further proof of the durability of the British designs.

The *Formidable* was hit again on 9 May - the

Admiral Sir Bruce Fraser adds his signature to the Japanese Instrument of Surrender, 2 September 1945. Behind him stands Rawlings, flanked by Brind and General Douglas MacArthur. A30425

day victory was being celebrated in Europe - and her sister *Victorious*, which had so far escaped the attentions of the kamikazes, was hit twice in a matter of minutes. Again, both ships sustained damage and casualties but remained operational. [11]

Throughout the rest of May the British continued their cycle of strikes and replenishment, with the battered *Formidable* being withdrawn for a refit on 22 May. The remaining three carriers flew their final attacks on 25 May, after which they turned back for Manus and then Sydney. On 27 May Spruance handed over to Admiral William 'Bull' Halsey, and TF57 became TF37. [12]

While the majority of the BPF was replenishing or refitting, Brind was given the task of 'breaking in' the newly arrived fleet carrier *Implacable* in a raid against Truk - formerly a powerful Japanese base, but now in effect a soft target. [13]

The battle for Okinawa had meanwhile entered its final phase, though the death on 18 June of the American ground force commander, Lt General Buckner, testified to the ferocity of the fighting. Organised resistance was finally broken on 21 June, leaving the way clear to move against the Japanese home islands.

The British Pacific Fleet sailed from Sydney on 28 June to play its part in this next round of operations, though with only a single battleship (*Howe* having left the fleet to undergo a refit at Durban) and two carriers - the newly refitted *Formidable*, flying Vian's flag, and the *Victorious*. (*Indomitable* had left the fleet, her place taken by *Implacable*. *Indefatigable* was in dock having faults rectified; she rejoined on 20 July. Britain's other two modern battleships - *Anson* and *Duke of York* - were on their way from Europe, but neither would actually arrive in time to fire their guns in anger).

After picking up Brind's force at Manus, Rawlings's ships joined the 3rd Fleet early on 16 July some three hundred miles east of Japan. This time, instead of being given their own targets, the British achieved full integration into the American carrier force, now commanded by Vice-Admiral J S McCain. [14]

The following day the US and British carriers began a methodical series of strikes on the home islands, sailing up and down the east coast to launch their planes against airfields, ports and industrial plants. Occasionally the British also got the chance to pound coastal targets with their guns, as on 17/18 July, when *King George V* joined the US battleships *Missouri*, *Iowa*, *Wisconsin*, *Alabama* and *North Carolina* in delivering 2,000 tons of shells on the Hitachi area. [15]

On the evening of 10 August, frustratingly close to the planned withdrawal of the British for major replenishment, the Domei News Agency in Tokyo announced that Japan had offered to accept the terms of surrender outlined at Potsdam.

In order to keep at least a token British presence, Fraser directed Rawlings to leave behind a small group when the bulk of the BPF departed for Sydney. *King George V* (still flying Rawlings's flag), *Indefatigable*, *Newfoundland* (flying Brind's flag), *Gambia* and ten destroyers accordingly stayed on with Halsey for the final act. [16]

Confirmation that the Japanese had indeed accepted surrender terms arrived on 15 August, and on 27 August Halsey's fleet, its British task group now led by Fraser himself in the newly arrived *Duke of York*, anchored triumphantly in Sagami Bay.

The Pacific Post

The Royal Navy again hits the headlines. Not, on this occasion, by a brilliantly fought battle, a safely shepherded convoy, or participation in invasion. The Navy hits the headlines by producing them.

So began the press release announcing the first issue of the *Pacific Post*, the daily paper of the British Pacific Fleet, which ran from Friday 20 July until 30 November 1945, and was, as the first editorial claimed, the Royal Navy's 'first newspaper - written and edited and printed by men of the Navy for men in the Navy'.

The idea for the paper originated with Sir Bruce Fraser, who realised that 'boredom was probably a greater enemy than the Jap.....and that the best way to conquer the loneliness of the greatest ocean on earth was

Accompanied by Willis (extreme left) and Kimmins, Admiral Sir Bruce Fraser takes over from the operator to start the *Pacific Post* presses rolling on 20 July 1945. A29854

Midshipman Ronald Robson and Admiral Sir Bruce Fraser with the first issue of *Pacific Post*. A 29855

The staff of *Pacific Post* photographed towards the end of the paper's life. Seated in the sceond row (left to right) are Ernest Petts, Eric Leppard, Ted Glover, John Willis, Don Newton and Stan Wasson, together with secretaries and ratings.

Daily Newspaper of the British Pacific Fleet

PACIFIC POST

No. 1—DUMMY RUN   WEDNESDAY JULY 18, 1945   FREE TO THE FLEET

TODAY...

Wednesday, July 18, 1945

THIS newspaper makes history. It is the Navy's first newspaper — written, edited, and printed by men of the Navy for the men in the Navy.

Our small staff is composed of printers, compositors, artists, and journalists who have been pulled out of ships of the British Pacific Fleet and elsewhere in order to give you a daily newspaper. Most of the staff have seen action from the Atlantic and the Arctic, the Channel and the Mediterranean, out to the Pacific. It is right that you should know this.

Pacific Post is your newspaper. It has no political axes to grind, and no one to serve except you in the Fleet. If you do not like it, say so; if you do, tell us just the same.

Like the British Pacific Fleet itself, we are facing terrific difficulties of communications in attempting to get this newspaper to you. No newspaper in the world prints so far from its readers. Most of the time you will be four thousand miles away from the presses of Pacific Post. A Fleet of aircraft will form the newspaper train that brings this paper to you. Destroyers and ships of the Fleet Train will be your news boys. So that while you are at sea it will certainly be impossible to give you the current news as promptly as we could wish.

But what we aim to do is to give you the gossip from home, the news you want to know above all the screaming headlines and echoes of war. The news from Rockmundwike and Harrow, Glasgow and Penrith—the little items that fall through the net of the cable correspondents but which, to the men in the ships, so many thousands of miles from home, conjure up pictures of unimportant places where very important people live. Such things like as the news of the Villa's new half-back; a new greyhound record at White City; the betting on the Caesarewitch and the England "test" team. A special news service by cable and wireless will provide this daily feature.

A well-informed correspondent sends a weekly sketch from the House of Commons. The writer is a serviceman and will pay particular attention to matters affecting those in the armed forces. And every day the writer of this column will comment as impartially as any one can do, on the events of the day in Britain and abroad.

The birth of a newspaper is always important. It is usually an evidence of commercial acumen in discovering a potential market for a particular commodity. Sometimes it is a political pregnancy. Rarely is it conceived in such a spirit of altruism as is Pacific Post. No advertiser and no shareholder is responsible for its appearance on your mess decks and in your wardrooms. It is your paper.

War Report

British in Vast Blows on Tokyo

A BRITISH task force, which includes the battleship King George V and the aircraft-carrier Formidable, has begun attacks on the Japanese homeland.

Combined British and American Fleets, pounding at the Tokyo area, have launched carrier blows in great strength, and at the time of going to press, the attacks were continuing.

Admiral Nimitz, in revealing this, stated that the two fleets represented the most formidable naval force ever gathered in the Pacific.

The Anglo-American force probably hurled about 1,500 carrier planes into the Tokyo area. Tokyo radio said the force included ten carriers.

Support for this report is given by the news that Vice-Admiral Sir Philip Vian is commanding the carrier force. Only carrier announced by name is H.M.S. Formidable.

Vice-Admiral Sir Bernard Rawlings is in tactical command of the British force, which includes the cruisers Black Prince and Newfoundland, the destroyers Barfleur, Grenville, Troubridge and Undine, in addition to the Australian destroyer Quickmish.

Corsairs and other aircraft rocket-strafed Kushira airfield, Southern Kyushu, destroying barracks, buildings and parked aircraft.

These blows, the first combined operations against the Japanese homeland, followed the blasted week in Japan's history.

Seen by Mr. Churchill in his tour of ruined Berlin—the Borsig Palace, on the Wilhelmstrasse, which Hitler used as his residence in Berlin.

Mystery Shrouds Opening of Potsdam Conference

SECRECY enveloped the converted Hohenzollern family home at Potsdam, as the stage was set for the conference of the Big Three, which is to formulate a common Allied policy for Germany.

One Berlin report dramatically stated that the conference between Mr. Churchill, President Truman, and Generalissimo Stalin had already begun, after Moscow Radio had given the first news of the arrival of Generalissimo Stalin and the Soviet Foreign Commissar, M. Molotov.

Until the Moscow announcement, correspondents were told nothing of the Soviet leaders' arrival, and it was impossible to gain any information regarding the schedule or agenda of the conference.

The mystery deepened when, following the Moscow broadcast the chief of the Russian Information Service in Berlin declared that he had no news of the arrival of Stalin and Molotov.

An Amgot spokesman stated that opening of the full scale conference had apparently met with some delay, and that the first meeting of the Big Three was expected to take place at any moment.

A few hours before there was still no official news of the whereabouts of the Soviet leaders, who reportedly left Moscow for Potsdam on Sunday.

It is, however, assumable (says "Times," that Stalin has arrived, as there has been considerable relaxation in precautions.

Premier and Truman Meet

Before the conference started Mr. Churchill visited President Truman in Potsdam for informal talks. The Anglo-American Chiefs of Staff also assembled for their first preliminary discussion.

The "Times" Diplomatic correspondent stated that the large number of Generals, Admirals and Air Force Officers which had accompanied the Allied leaders to Potsdam and the presence of the British Minister of War Transport, Lord Leathers, caused some surprise, it being asked whether the Pacific War and the Soviet policy thereon will be examined.

The Japanese certainly fear that the recent Soviet denunciation of its Russo-Japanese Treaty of Friendship may have a recurring sequel.

TOMMY CUTS RED TAPE

BRITISH Tommies broke through the red tape recently when they marched with fixed bayonets on to the Berlin Airfield. Surprised Russian guards raised previously closed barriers to let them through.

No international incident was caused and none is likely to develop.

The Tommies' action broke all no official news of the whereabouts of the Soviet leaders, who reportedly left Moscow for Potsdam on Sunday.

As time drew short, the Grenadiers fixed bayonets, sloped arms and marched in—and the Russian guards raised no objection.

TYPHUS IN VIENNA

Only Twelve Food Lorries

Visiting Paris en route for London and Washington, Jean Lambert, personal representative of the head of the Austrian provisional government, drew a dark picture of the situation in Vienna.

He said that typhus has broken out in the city, where children were playing on infested rubbish heaps. Rubbish could not be moved from the streets through lack of transport—only twelve municipal lorries were available for food distribution.

—M.A.P.

BERLINERS AMAZED AT CHURCHILL

BERLINERS gave Mr. Churchill an amazing welcome when he startled everybody by strolling through the wrecked and looted Chancellory, where Hitler's body was reported to have been burned.

All the Germans who saw him wanted to fraternise with him (says the "Daily Mail" Berlin correspondent.

They waved, smiled, and had to be forced back by military policemen, otherwise they would have mobbed him as a hero.

As soon as they realised his identity, they crowded in upon him, and apparently could hardly believe their eyes that it was Mr. Churchill they saw walking through the ruins.

We who were watching also found it hard to believe that the Germans would ever be pleased to see Mr. Churchill, yet here they were smiling and exclaiming excitedly "Churchill!" as he passed.

But Mr. Churchill had no smiles for the Berliners. He chewed firmly upon the inevitable cigar, and was obviously in a dour mood.

"Bond Street Stroll"

It was an extraordinary sensation, (says the "Daily Telegraph's" Berlin correspondent) to see Mr. Churchill, bitterest foe of Nazism, the most hated man in Germany, walking the streets among a Berlin crowd with only a couple of detectives and a handful of military police for guard.

He was as much at ease as though strolling Bond Street, though the shift he ran must have crossed the minds of most of those present.

Mr. Churchill was accompanied by his daughter Mary, Mr. Anthony Eden, Sir Alexander Cadogen (Foreign Office) and Sir Archibald Clark Kerr (Ambassador to Moscow).

He was met at Brandenburg Gate by the Russian Military Governor, Colonel-General Gorbatov. The Premier struck an almost belligerent pose while standing near the spot where Hitler is said to have died.

He spent about half-an-hour stalking swiftly through the famed buildings in rubble, and frequently poking with his stick among the debris.

"Terrible"—President

President Truman also visited the devastated heart of Berlin and the ruined Chancellory. Unlike Mr. Churchill, however, he did not alight.

As his car stopped outside the Chancellory, the President shook his head and remarked: "It is a terrible thing, but they brought it on themselves. It demonstrates what man does when he overreaches himself."

The President's car was preceded by an armoured escort.

(Messages from A.A.P.)

WAR CRIMES TRIAL CONFESSION

Two German policemen confessed before a military court to the murder of a young American airman shot down near Hanau last December.

One of the accused men, Wilhelm Haefner, said that when the airman was brought into the local police station he took him before the local chief of police, who quoted instructions from higher authority that "Allied fliers guilty of terror attacks should no longer be treated as prisoners of war."

Haefner calmly described to the court how, in company with two other policemen, he took the American a short distance from the village and shot him through the head.

Trial of Haefner and his associates is proceeding.

—M.A.P.

No. 1 Dummy Run of *Pacific Post* leads with the opening of the Potsdam Conference and Churchill's tour of the devastated German capital.
Berliners, 'except for one old man who shook his head disapprovingly, all began to cheer... I was much moved by their demonstrations,' recorded the Prime Minister.

to get news from home to the men in the Fleet with least possible delay.' At Fraser's request a series of publications was planned and Lieutenant John Willis RNVR, in London, was told; 'Pack your bags, you're going to start a newspaper for the British Pacific Fleet.' Willis had served for two years on a minesweeper in 'E-Boat Alley' before obtaining a commission at HMS *King Alfred*. He then went on to assist Commander Tommy Woodrooffe in producing the Royal Navy's magazine *Ditty Box*, a task for which he was well suited as he had been assistant editor of *Everybody's Weekly* before joining the Navy in February 1942. Among the innovations that he brought to the production of *Ditty Box* was the introduction of glamorous 'pin-up' girls. As it was His Majesty's Stationary Office which published *Ditty Box*, along with its more usual staid fare of Government White Papers and Blue Books, Willis claimed 'with some pride, to be the first man to put a pin-up girl in a Stationary Office publication'.

Willis arrived in Australia early in 1945, and obtained from Captain Anthony Kimmins RN, the wartime naval commentator, then serving as Chief of Naval Information (Pacific), permission to recruit his staff from ships and establishments in all parts of the Pacific. Although this policy had the blessing of Admiral Fraser 'many a commanding officer and Drafting Officer found it difficult to agree that in war the pen could ever be as mighty as the sword.' Nonetheless, Willis was adamant that 'if the Navy is to have a newspaper, then it must be run like newspaper and not like a ship', and so experienced journalists now serving in the Navy were sought and obtained.

One such was Lieutenant (S) Frank Eyles RNVR, who had come out from Britain on the liner *Empress of Scotland* at the end of 1944 to join the staff of Flag Officer Naval Air Stations, Australia. Mr Eyles recalls:

> I found myself faced with the drudgery of the work I had been doing for a similar office at Lee on Solent: the production and distribution of command standing orders and memoranda etc. This continued for some weeks until I saw my chance of release from the boredom in a general signal sent to ships and establishments by the C-in-C Pacific Fleet. This called for volunteers with newspaper production experience to make up the staff of *Pacific Post* which was to be printed in Sydney and delivered daily to units of the fleet.

Having worked before the war for both the *Chichester Observer* and the *Portsmouth Evening News* I was warmly welcomed by Lieutenant John Willis RNVR.

Another recruit was Sub-Lieutenant Don Newton who had been on the staff of the *South Wales Argus* and the *Western Gazette* as well as Chairman of the Exeter Branch of the National Union of Journalists. Prior to his posting to Australia, Sub-Lieutenant Newton had served as a member of the liaison crew of the Dutch frigate *Johan Maurits*. In Australia he was serving at a naval air station on the outskirts of Sydney when Willis asked him if he would care to join the staff of Fleet Publications which was to produce *Pacific Post*. Mr Newton recalled:

> Would I? Would any journalist have missed such a chance? I jumped at it, then went back to persuade my CO that I would be of far more use to the Navy helping to produce a newspaper than I would be in his Signals Office, but he was not easily convinced.

If Messrs Newton and Eyles were experienced journalists, some of the other volunteers, Mr Eyles recalls, 'had rather less than the expertise they claimed. Their motive was to get away from the fighting ships and the war against Japan to safety and luxury in Sydney. This was particularly true of one or two of the mechanical staff, but they proved quick learners at setting and casting type, and I don't think we ever had to boot anyone out for incompetence.'

Originally, it was intended that 'Fleet Publications', based at the Sydney offices of the Truth and Sportsman publishing firm on Pitt Street, would not only bring out the daily *Pacific Post* with a special magazine edition on Sundays, but also two magazines, *Up Spirits* and *Fleet Parade*. The former was to adopt the format of *Men Only*, the latter that of Edward Hulton's hugely successful *Picture Post*, Britain's leading magazine throughout the war years and beyond. Don Newton comments: 'It was an ambitious plan, but as Japan collapsed at a much earlier date than was expected, the two magazines were abandoned.'

Pacific Post, however, soon went ahead. Frank Eyles was made responsible for the design and production of the news pages, also doing much of the sub-editing and headline writing with the help of two or three others including Coder Len Fugue (who had been a *Daily Herald* sub-editor), and Air Mechanic Walter Craig. Don Newton, also an assistant editor, was responsible for features, while Sub-Lieutenant Ted Glover RNVR was sports editor. Although Truth and Sportsman supplied a

Daily Newspaper of the British Pacific Fleet

PACIFIC POST

No. 9   SATURDAY, JULY 28, 1945   FREE TO THE FLEET

ATTLEE (390 SEATS) FORMS HIS GOVERNMENT

WHILE Britain and all the world was expressing amazement yesterday at the Labour landslide in the general election, Mr. Attlee, the new Prime Minister, was forming the new Government.

As soon as the result was beyond doubt, Mr. Churchill went to the Palace, and handed his resignation to the King. Shortly afterward, Mr. Attlee was summoned and invited to take office.

Final figures—with the exception of 12 university seats, to come later, and Central Hull where polling was delayed through a candidate's death—show that Labour has won 390 of 627 seats, Conservatives 196, Liberal National 14, Liberals 11, Independents 10, I.L.P. 3, Communist 2, National 1, and Common Wealth 1.

The totals mean that the Government secured 210 seats and the Opposition 417. The Conservative Party lost 182 seats and gained seven while Labour had 215 gains and four losses.

Mr. Churchill's Government was virtually wiped out for twenty-nine Ministers, including the three Service Ministers—Mr. Brendan Bracken (Navy), Sir James Grigg (War), and Mr. Harold MacMillan (Air)—were defeated.

Other "casualties" in the Government ranks were Mr. Amery (India), Sir Walter Womersley (Pensions), Mr. Geoffrey Lloyd (Information), Colonel Llewellin (Food), Mr. Richard Law (Education), Mr. Hore-Belisha (Insurance) and Mr. Ernest Brown (Aircraft Production).

Both Mr. Churchill's son, Major Randolph Churchill, and his son-in-law Mr. Duncan Sandys, were beaten.

Women's Best Yet

Mr. Churchill will still have the support of many powerful colleagues on the Opposition Bench. They include Eden, Lyttelton, Stanley, Butler, Hudson, Duncan, Willink, and Crookshank.

Twenty-three women have been elected—the highest number in the history of Parliament. They are all labour except Viscountess Davidson (Cons.) and Lady Megan Lloyd George (Liberal).

Jennie Lee (Aneurin Bevan's wife) returns to Parliament after a long absence with a majority of 19,634.

Some candidates slipped in with the narrowest of margins. George Ward (Cons) had a margin of four at Worcester; Gandar Dower six at Caithness; and Brigadier Foster fifteen at Northwich. H. L. Hutchinson won Rusholme (Manchester) for Labour by ten votes.—A.A.P.

Mr. Attlee, Britain's new Prime Minister. He expects to form a Government at once, and then return to Potsdam.

WHAT THE PARTY LEADERS SAID

"BRITAIN FACING A NEW ERA" — Mr. Attlee

"WE are facing a new era, and I believe the result shows that the people of Britain are facing it with the same courage that they have faced the six years of war."

So said MR. ATTLEE, Britain's new leader, in his statement after Labour's sweeping victory.

The people have made up their minds regarding the kind of policy they want to see, both at home and in foreign policy, and I am confident that Labour can deliver the goods. My colleagues and I fully realise the magnitude of the task facing us.

"We have never swerved from our position of the need for a new world order for the prevention of war. Equally, we have a new world policy which is based on the endeavour to raise the standards of life for the masses throughout the world. Our home policy is in consonance with our foreign policy.

"I think the electors understand that policy, and realise that Labour has the will and men to carry it out.

"Spirit of New Age"

"Labour is fortunate in having a fine lot of candidates, including a great many young servicemen, who will bring into the Commons the spirit of the new age.

"I believe we are on the eve of a great advance in the human race that will mean not only work here, but above all, the co-operation of other nations, particularly our great Allies, Russia and America."

Liberal Leader's Hope

SIR ARCHIBALD SINCLAIR, leader of the Liberal Party who was defeated after holding Caithness and Sutherland for twenty-three years, said:

"The Liberal Party has done badly, but we polled over two million votes, and every constituency where the Liberal candidate fought reported a tremendous accession of new workers. This promises to provide a firm basis for future operations."

Mr. HERBERT MORRISON, Chairman of the Labour campaign committee, declared that Labour succeeded in putting the issues clearly before the public, whereas the Conservatives tried to convert the election into a plebiscite for and against Mr Churchill.

"I denounced that as something in the nature of imitation Nazism, and I think the country proved that it regarded it in the same way."

MR. EDEN—"I deeply regret the national decision, but accept it because I believe in democracy."

Admiral Lord Louis Mountbatten, Supreme Commander of South East Asia Command, arriving in Britain after attending the Big Three Conference in Potsdam. Here he is seen greeting his daughter, Wren Third Officer Patricia. Lady Louis Mountbatten is on the right. (Picture by Baum)

NAZI SHELLS FOR JAPS

Nearly a million tons of German ammunition, which the Allies captured, will be used to help beat Japan, says a U.S. Ordnance statement.—A.A.P.

Churchill's Message

Mr. Churchill's statement on the result was as follows:—

"The decision of the British people has been recorded. I have, therefore, laid down the charge which was placed upon me in darker times. I regret I have not been permitted to finish the work against Japan.

"For this, however, all plans and preparations have been made, and results may come much quicker than we have hitherto been entitled to expect.

"Immense responsibilities, abroad and at home, fall on the new Government, and we must all hope they will be successful in bearing them.

"It only remains for me to express to the British people, for whom I have acted in these perilous years, my profound gratitude for the unflinching and unwavering support which they have given me during my task, and for the many expressions of kindness which they have shown towards their servant."

Labour Tribute

Professor Harold Laski, on behalf of the Labour Party, thanked Mr. Churchill for the great services he had rendered to the nation as Premier.

"This is a hard night for Mr. Churchill," he said, "but it is not of our making. It is the British people who have spoken, and we thank them for the proof of the full maturity of British democracy."—A.A.P.

NOT TO RETURN TO POTSDAM?

The result caused a sensation among delegates at Potsdam, and there was much speculation as to what would happen when the conference was resumed.

First impression was that Mr. Attlee would extend to Mr. Churchill an invitation to return as a member of the delegation, but few seemed to think he would accept it.

It is believed that Mr. Attlee may return within two or three days, but, failing that, the conference recess will become a formal adjournment.

Home opinion, too, is that Mr. Churchill will not return. Mr. Bevin may accompany Mr. Attlee (says the "Daily Express").—A.A.P.

THREE JAP CITIES SET ON FIRE

GUAM, Friday—The Allied offensive against Japan was continued yesterday when 350 Superfortresses dropped 2,200 tons of incendiaries on three Japanese industrial cities.

The targets raided were Omuta, on Kyushu Island, one of Japan's most important chemical centres; Matsuyama, important port on western Shikoku Island; and Tokuyama, a chemical centre on Honshu.

Admiral Nimitz's communique reveals that marine aircraft bombed and rocket-strafed radio stations on Amami Island in the Ryukyus. Privateers sank three and damaged five fishing vessels south of Tokyo Bay.

When Jap torpedo planes attacked units of the U.S. Third Fleet, planes from British carriers broke up the attack (says a correspondent aboard the American flagship).

Four Jap planes were shot down, and the others fled after dropping their bombs harmlessly into the sea.

Heavy bombers from Okinawa ran into thirty enemy fighters over Kyushu areas. Seven of them were shot down, and one probably shot down, for the loss of one bomber.—A.A.P.

ALLIED TERMS TO JAPS

IMMEDIATE and unconditional surrender is demanded from Japan in a joint statement by Allied leaders, issued from Potsdam, and just announced.

The statement, made by Mr. Churchill, President Truman and Marshal Chiang Kai-Shek, says that prodigious land, sea and air forces are poised, ready to strike at Japan until she ceases to exist.

The announcement sets out terms for Japan's surrender, and points out that the time has come for Japan to decide whether she will choose annihilation or follow the path of reason.

Occupation of Japan

The terms set out include the occupation of whatever Japanese territory the Allies decide upon, and the limiting of Japanese sovereignty to the home islands of Honshu, Hokkaido, Kyushu and Shikoku, and such minor islands as the Allies determine.

All Japanese troops must be disarmed and returned to peaceful lives at home. War criminals, including those who visited cruelties upon our prisoners, must be punished.

It is not intended to enslave the Japanese people, and they must be allowed freedom of speech, religion and thought. Japan will not be allowed to maintain any industries which would enable her to rearm.

Surrender Demand

The statement said: "Occupying forces of the Allies shall be withdrawn from Japan as soon as these objectives have been accomplished, and there has been established in accordance with the freely expressed will of the Japanese people, a peacefully inclined and responsible Government.

"We call upon the Government of Japan to proclaim unconditional surrender of all Japanese armed forces, and provide for proper assurance of their good faith in such action.

"The alternative for Japan is complete and utter destruction."—A.A.P.

1,000 U.S. Troops Die In Jap Ship

Japan has informed the War Department in Washington that 942 American prisoners of war were killed outright when a prison ship was torpedoed in Subic Bay, in the Philippines, last December.

Another fifty-nine died later, and of 630 survivors, two escaped. The rest presumably were taken to Japan.

Tokio Radio says that Superfortresses bombed a prisoner-of-war camp at Kawasaki, on Wednesday, causing casualties among the prisoners, who were mostly Americans.—A.A.P.

Another Stage in Leopold Debate

After a week of wrangling over King Leopold, a vote of confidence in the Belgian Government was passed by ninety-nine votes to sixty-three, "approving entirely the position of the Government."

The Government made a condition that Leopold must not return without the approval of both Houses.—A.A.P.

LAVAL MAY RETURN TO PARIS

It is reliably learned (says Reuter from Barcelona) that Laval has applied to the Spanish authorities for his release from Montjuich Fortress. It is believed he intends to go to Paris at his own risk.—A.A.P.

Pacific Post announces Labour's victory in the 1945 General Election. Mrs Churchill's comment was 'It may well be a blessing in disguise.' To which Churchill replied 'At the moment it seems quite effectively disguised.'

Daily Newspaper of the British Pacific Fleet

PACIFIC POST

No. 28 THURSDAY, AUGUST 16, 1945 FREE TO THE FLEET

It was Mr. Attlee who broke the news to the waiting world that the—

WAR IS OVER
—THE JOB ISN'T

The Prime Minister's dramatic announcement, made at midnight (London time) on Tuesday brought to an end a flood of rumours. "Japan has surrendered," he said, ". . . but on Friday morning we must turn again to the great tasks which challenge us."

Throughout the day messages from Japan itself and from Switzerland, had foreshadowed the momentous event, but the Allied capitals kept the world in suspense until Mr. Attlee began his broadcast.

Hundreds of carrier 'planes which were on the point of bombing Tokyo were called back when the news reached Admiral Halsey.

Within a few minutes of Mr. Attlee going on the air singing and cheering crowds began parading the West End of London.

The news came on the eve of the State opening of the new Parliament.

Ships in Southampton Docks greeted the news with hooting sirens, the "Queen Mary" leading with repeated "V" signals from her deep-noted fog horn.

In Washington President Truman said: "I deem this reply a full acceptance of the Potsdam declaration, which specifies the unconditional surrender of Japan. In this reply there is no qualification."

He added that arrangements were now being made for the formal signing of the surrender terms.

General MacArthur has been appointed the Supreme Allied Commander to receive the surrender.

SYDNEY WENT WILD

AMAZING scenes of rejoicing were seen in Sydney Harbour, the main rear base of the British Pacific Fleet.

Naval discipline temporarily went by the board. Commanders and ratings linked hands and danced round bollards and over chains on the cable decks, while above the din from every ship's siren in the harbour, waves of cheering swept from ship to ship.

In H.M.S. Anson sailors climbed the crow's nest beneath with caps and cotton waste. The crews of two tiny tugs challenged "Anson" by loud hailer. "Anson" replied with her hosepipes and a water-battle developed.

"Pipe Down"

Officers and men of the Fleet on leave in Sydney joined in the vast crowds in Martin Place and other main streets. Some souvenir hunters collected their white caps.

Above the din of whistles and rattles some of the men who had brought their bosun's pipes, sounded "Pipe Down."

As soon as Truman proclaims the official V-J Day, U.S. newspaper, radio and mail censorship will cease.

"LAST OF OUR ENEMIES LAID LOW"

Great Britain, Russia, and China will be represented by high-ranking officers. In the meantime, the Allied armed forces have been ordered to suspend offensive action.

Proclamation of V-J Day will await the formal signing of the surrender terms by Japan.

Russians heard the news when Moscow radio flashed, "Japan surrendered unconditionally."

Canadian celebrations were in advance of the official news.

Police and marines dispersed a crowd of several thousands which converged on a liquor store in Victoria and hurled rocks through the windows.

Mr. Attlee began his broadcast with the words: "Japan has to-day surrendered. The last of our enemies is laid low. Here is the text of Japan's reply to the Allied terms:— '

The Japanese reply he announced was:—

"His Majesty the Emperor has issued an Imperial Rescript regarding Japan's acceptance of the provisions of the Potsdam declaration. The Emperor is prepared to authorise and ensure the signature by his Government and Imperial General Headquarters of necessary terms for carrying out the provisions of the Potsdam declaration. The Emperor is also prepared to issue a command to Japanese Military, Naval and Air Forces and all Forces under their control, wherever they may be found, to cease all active operations, relinquish all arms and obey all commands by the Allied Forces in accordance with the above terms."

"Surprise and Treachery"

Mr. Attlee went on: "Let us recall that on December 7, 1941, Japan whose onslaught China had resisted for over four years fell upon America, who were not then at war and ourselves who were sore pressed, in our death struggles with Germany and Italy.

"Taking full advantage of surprise and treachery, the Japanese forces quickly overran the territories of ourselves and our Allies in the Far East, and at one time it appeared that these invaders would reach the mainland of Australia, and advance into India.

"Tide Turned"

"But the tide turned, at first slowly and then with ever-increasing speed and violence, and with the mighty forces which the United States, the British Commonwealth and Empire, all their Allies, and finally Russia brought to bear, their resistance everywhere has now been broken.

"At this time we should pay tribute to the men of this country, the Dominions, India and the Colonies, to our fleets, armies and air forces, who fought so well in the arduous campaign.

"Our gratitude goes out to all our splendid Allies, and above all, to the United States, without whose prodigious efforts the war in the East would still have many years to run.

"CONTINUED" ... "LAST OF OUR ENEMIES LAID LOW"

(Continued on page 4, col. 4)

Japs Get Orders

THE following message was sent to the Japanese Government by President Truman:—

"You are to proceed as follows —(1) Direct the prompt cessation of hostilities by Japanese forces, informing the Supreme Commander for the Allied Powers of the effective date and hour of such cessation.

"(2) Send emissaries at once to the Supreme Commander with information of the disposition of Japanese forces and commanders and with full powers to make any arrangements directed by the Supreme Commander to enable him and his accompanying forces to arrive at the place designated by him to receive formal surrender.

(3) For the purpose of receiving such surrender and of carrying it into effect, General Douglas MacArthur has been designated as Supreme Commander for the Allied Powers, and he will notify the Japanese Government of a time, place and other details of the formal surrender.

"Why We Gave In"—Hirohito

Hirohito, in a broadcast to the Japanese people, said that both fighting services and civilians had done their best, but the enemy had begun to use a new and most cruel bomb.

They, therefore, had accepted the ultimatum against continuance of the war under the conditions which would have resulted not only in the ultimate collapse and obliteration of the Japanese people, but would also have led to the total extinction of human civilisation.

"We have resolved to pave the way for a great peace for all generations to come by enduring the unendurable and suffering what is insufferable," he said.

VJ Day in London announced by *Pacific Post*. Diarist James Lees-Milne records 'I am strangely unmoved by the announcement. The world is left a victim of chaos, great uncertainty and heinous turpitude.'

Daily Newspaper of the British Pacific Fleet

PACIFIC POST

No. 134 FRIDAY, NOVEMBER 30, 1945 FREE TO THE FLEET

TODAY

Friday, November 30, 1945.

With this issue "Pacific Post" ceases publication. Normally, a newspaper dies for the good and sufficient reason that it is failing to show a profit, because it has neither the support (nor the revenue) of its readers and advertisers.

"Pacific Post" dies for a different reason. It has been edited, printed, and published in Sydney—until now the main base of the British Pacific Fleet. Victory over Japan has meant a progressive movement of ships and men from Australia to Hong Kong and Singapore. And that same victory has meant that other ships and men are returning to the United Kingdom.

Singapore is nearly 4,000 miles from our presses, Hong Kong even farther. It has been taking us an average of five days by air to bring you your "Pacific Post."

☆ ☆ ☆

"SEAC," the daily newspaper of South East Asia Command, which was a veteran in the Forces' newspaper field before "Pacific Post" was born, begins publication from Singapore tomorrow. "SEAC," like "Pacific Post," prints world and home news, but "SEAC" — because it will be produced almost on your doorstep—will reach most of you within twenty-four hours of its leaving the presses.

And so "Pacific Post" dies because "SEAC" can bring you the news from home with a minimum of delay.

Over to you, "SEAC."

☆ ☆ ☆

Without the willing help, the generous co-operation of many people, both in Australia and at home, "Pacific Post" could not have been produced. We wish to say a very sincere "thank you" to the directors of Messrs. Truth and Sportsman, "Sydney Morning Herald," Consolidated Press, Associated Newspapers, Australian Associated Press, Yaffa Syndicate, Newspaper Supplies, Associated Wireless (Australasia), "Daily Mirror" (London), Reuter, Press Association, and Mr. Kerwin Maegraith.

J.W.

COURT HEARS STORY OF AUSTRIA'S FALL

LONDON, Thursday.—The War Crimes Tribunal, at their seventh session in Nuremberg, heard the full story of the annexation of Austria, where, said the prosecution, the "first flower" of the Fifth Column was seen.

With heavy rain falling outside, and only a glimmer of grey light showing through the curtained windows of the Palace of Justice, more arc lights, brighter than ever, were turned on the Nazi war-leaders in the dock.

A huge chart showing how the occupation of Austria led to open war was prominently displayed as the deputy American prosecutor, Mr. Sidney Alderman, began to tell the story of Austria's fall.

He said the acquisition of Austria was a Nazi aim from 1933.

He read an affidavit by Mr. G. S. Messersmith, American diplomat formerly stationed in Berlin and Vienna, who said that when he was in Vienna, the former Chancellors, Dollfuss and Von Schuschnigg, and President Miklas, told him the Nazis were applying continuous pressure to gain places in the Cabinet, after which they intended to crush all opposition from inside.

The Nazis resorted to economic pressure, propaganda, and terroristic acts to compel the Austrian Government to accept their terms.

Secret Visits to Hitler

Nazi officials in Berlin had told him that outrages were instigated and directed by them, but when Hitler visited Mussolini in Venice in mid-June, 1934, the outrages momentarily stopped, as Mussolini was supporting the Austrian Government and Hitler could not afford an open break with Mussolini then.

The affidavit recounted intrigues and accused Seyss-Inquart, who was Chancellor of Austria for three days before the annexation, and who later became Governor of Holland.

Seyss-Inquart was said to have deceived Schuschnigg by professing a great friendship, while making secret visits to Hitler.

The affidavit concluded: "In 1938, satisfied that Britain and France would not, and knowing that Italy could not, take action, Hitler struck the final blow at Austrian independence, bringing to a climax what must be recorded as one of the most insidious, dastardly, unjustified, and altogether effective series of measures to bring about the end of a sovereign state."

Goering Looked Angry

Goering became excited, loudly saying: "Nein, nein," and writing rapidly as Mr. Alderman sketched events in Vienna on July 25, 1934, when Dollfuss was murdered.

Goering, for the first time during the trial, looked angry as Mr. Alderman said the Austrian "putsch" was organised by German and Austrian Nazis.

Mr. Alderman submitted the trial's first photographic evidence—a picture of the plaque the Germans erected in Vienna in 1938 to the killers of Dollfuss—and added: "The inscription shows that Nazi Germany took the responsibility and the credit for the death of Dollfuss."

Von Papen shook his head vigorously when Mr. Alderman requoted Messer-

(Continued in col. 2, page 4)

COMMONS CONCERN OVER R. A. F. ACCIDENT RATE

INQUIRY REFUSED

LONDON, Thursday. — Wing Commander Strachey, Under-Secretary for Air, refused a public inquiry into recent accidents to Transport Command aircraft after Sir William Wakefield had drawn attention in the Commons to what he described as "great public anxiety regarding the number of accidents."

Wing Commander Strachey gave an assurance that "very active measures for diminishing the rate of accidents" were now under consideration.

"Meteor" Still Missing

In a written reply he announced that forty-five passengers and fifteen crewmen were killed, and eleven passengers and one crew-man injured during November in three accidents involving passenger-carrying aircraft of Transport Command.

He also told the Commons that the Meteor aircraft which took off from Molesworth airfield on November 20 had still not been traced.—A.A.P.

Wouldn't Carry Hitler's Head

LONDON, Thursday.—£14,500 was realised yesterday at the resumed sale of furniture from the German Embassy, says the "Daily Mail."

Two haulage contractors refused to remove the 5 cwt. bust of Hitler's head, bought by Captain Gordon Canning for £500.

Insured for £750, it had to remain the night in the sale-room.—A.A.P.

Toys, Gifts For Britain

LONDON, Thursday.—A department called "Overseas Gifts Allocation Centre" has been established at Colwyn Bay to distribute Christmas gifts and toys on their way from the Dominions and elsewhere.

No gifts have yet been received, says the "Daily Mail," but quantities are on their way from Adelaide, Tasmania, New South Wales, Kenya, Argentine, South Africa, and other places.—A.A.P.

"China Must Solve Own Problem"

LONDON, Thursday.—The Foreign Minister, Mr. Ernest Bevin, in a reply to a question in the House of Commons, said that the Government regarded the civil war in China as an internal problem for the Chinese themselves to solve.

"Although there is no evidence that British trade and interests are so far directly affected, I am most anxious to see a settlement reached," he added.

Dispute "Narrows"

LONDON, Thursday. — Mr. George Isaacs told the Commons in reference to the docks' dispute, that the issue between the men and the employers was now narrowed to a matter of some shillings.

He said he was appointing a Committee to examine the situation, and hoped they would report in two or three days. —A.A.P.

"Labour Strangling Britain"

—MR. CHURCHILL.

LONDON, Thursday.—Telling a general conference of the Conservative Party that the vote at the last election was "one of the greatest disasters that has smitten this country," Mr. Churchill said:—"There is no reason why we shouldn't lead our country out of this foolish lapse and error, just as we led the country through the great world struggle."

"Happily, we have not got to fight a foreign foe, but only to regain the goodwill and revive the morale of our fellow countrymen."

Mr. Churchill said he had hoped the Government would have devoted itself to the task of liberating Britain from the thraldom of wartime. Instead, people were being harried and harrassed with vaguely thought-out and physically unobtainable plans.

Cripps Slated

He accused Labour of hampering and delaying the recovery of Britain for its own Party ends. From every quarter he had heard how enterprise was divided and fettered, queues and faces were longer, and forms and officials more plentiful.

"We are told that everything must be concentrated on exports," he said. "But whoever, outside an infant school or a lunatic asylum, would say that exports should not be the overspilling of successful home trade?"

Referring to Sir Stafford Cripps as "a great advocate of strength through misery," Mr. Churchill added: "He tried this theme on the Government in 1942. I didn't like it. I prefer strength through victory."—A.A.P.

DEATH SENTENCE FOR AMERY: 8-MINUTE TRIAL

LONDON, Thursday.—John Amery (33), son of Mr. L. S. Amery, former Secretary for India, was sentenced to death at the Old Bailey, yesterday, for high treason and treachery.

Amery pleaded guilty on all counts. The proceedings lasted only eight minutes.

His face was expressionless as he leaned forward and grasped the ledge of the dock and told the judge with a firm voice, "I plead guilty on all counts."

The judge warned Amery that he never accepted the plea of "Guilty" without assuring himself that the accused thoroughly understood what the result must be and the accused was thoroughly in accord with it.

"A Self-confessed Traitor"

Amery's legal advisor, Mr. G. O. Slade, said, "I give that assurance. I have explained the position fully to my client and I am satisfied that he understands."

After passing the sentence, Mr. Justice Humphreys said: "You have forfeited the right to live. You now stand a self-confessed traitor to your King and country."

Looking self-possessed as he heard the sentence, Amery bowed deeply to the judge and walked to the cells without showing any signs of emotion.

The public showed little interest in the trial. Only four women and sixteen men, including Amery's brother, watched the proceedings.—A.A.P.

Vast Sums For Electricity Plan

LONDON, Thursday.—Electricity generating stations throughout the country are embarking on a programme which will cost £150,000,000 over the next five years, said Mr. Harold Hobson, chairman of the Central Electricity Board, speaking in London.

Completion of the programme would result, he said, in an increased output of electricity of between eight and ten thousand million units a year, of which probably more than half would be for use in homes.

At least double the sum of £150,000,000 would be spent on transmission and distribution.—A.A.P.

AUTOGRAPH-HUNTERS CHASE THE COMMANDER-IN-CHIEF

SYDNEY, Thursday.—The esteem of Australians for Admiral Sir Bruce Fraser was much in evidence this afternoon, at the British Centre, in Hyde Park, when a special meeting was held to say farewell to the Commander-in-Chief.

After being repeatedly applauded throughout the meeting, and presented with a painting of Sydney Harbour, by Albert Collins, Sir Bruce was surrounded by eager autograph-hunters as he left.

Sir Bruce, who had expressed a wish that he might have an opportunity of personally thanking "all those friends who had worked so hard in the various sections of the Centre," said in an address that he was always happy in the British Centre.

He said the Royal Navy owed a tremendous debt of gratitude to the women of Australia.

Speaking of the move to Hong Kong, Sir Bruce explained that it was for purely geographical reasons.

"I have to move my ships north to where we shall be working—some 4,000 miles away," he remarked. "We shall have ships coming to Australia for the next six months—in fact I have the greatest difficulty in getting my men away from Sydney."

A tribute to the "courteousness and exemplary character of the thousands of men of the Royal Navy who have accepted the hospitality of Australians" was paid in the annual report of the British Centre, presented at the meeting.

LUXURY FLYING BOAT

LONDON, Thursday.—A new luxury flying boat, the "Sandringham," which will operate on the British Overseas Airways Corporation Empire routes, was launched today at Rochester, Kent.

Dachau Guards Deny Charges

DAUCHAU (Germany), Thursday.—The defence opened their case for the forty Dachau guards today, moving for "Not guilty" verdicts on the grounds that the charges did not show any common design by the accused.

The motions were rejected and the defence called Martin Weiss, camp commandant, who claimed that he introduced a number of reforms at Dachau and unsuccessfully argued with Himmler about the medical experiments made on prisoners.—A.A.P.

AUSTRIAN CABINET OUT

VIENNA, Thursday.—The Cabinet has placed its resignation in the hands of Renner and his political council.

The council has asked the Government to remain in office until Parliament meets on December 18, and has requested the Catholic People's Party to try and form a new government in the meantime.—A.A.P.

FAMOUS PROFESSOR IS ILL

LONDON, Thursday.—Eighty-years-old Professor Gilbert Murray, one of Britain's foremost experts on international affairs, and co-president of the League of Nations Union, who entered a nursing home at Oxford when he injured his back in a fall on November 5, is now suffering from pernicious anaemia, pneumonia and pleurisy.—A.A.P.

CALCUTTA RIOTS

CALCUTTA, Thursday.—One American was killed and 106 British and American military personnel were injured during demonstrations against the trial of the three officers from the Jap-sponsored "Indian National Army."

The final issue of *Pacific Post*, 30 November 1945, leads with the Nuremberg War Crimes Trial which had opened ten days before. Also featured is the trial of John Amery, who had attempted to raise the 'Legion of St. George' amongst British prisoners of war in Germany to fight the Russians. Amery, who had also broadcast for the Germans, was hanged on 19 December 1945.

handful of staff that included two print overseers, Eric Leppard and Stan Wasson, the rest of the staff - Linotype operators, stereotypers, proof-readers etc. - were all Royal Naval ratings.

Much of the material used for the *Pacific Post* was sent out by the Admiralty, reaching Fleet Publications in the form of teleprinter messages. There was naturally a large emphasis on 'local' stories - the only newspapers to reach the fleet from England were weeks old, and they tended to be the national dailies - and much of the material was channelled through the Naval Information and Liaison Division (NILDIV) in Sydney, which was also the source of the paper's photographs and stories from the Pacific Fleet itself.

Admiral Sir Bruce Fraser himself came to the *Pacific Post's* offices to start the presses for the first issue on 20 July 1945 (a run of some 20,000 copies). The Admiral jokingly commented 'I enjoyed myself very much. It is the first time in my life that I have not felt nervous with pressmen!' As the first copies of the paper were coming off the machines, a BBC Home Service announcement of the paper's inception was heard in the newsroom. Sir Bruce - a wonderful character, recalls Mr Eyles - remained for a party and was photographed holding the first issue with Midshipman R Robson RNVR of the publishing press.

Although the first issue claimed '*Pacific Post* is your newspaper. It has no political axes to grind and no one to serve except you in the Fleet', Frank Eyles recollects:

> In his determination to make *Pacific Post* look like a real newspaper, Willis made us print a daily 'leader' which he invariably wrote himself. I thought this might be asking for trouble, and sure enough he put his foot in it at least once with some sentiments which were regarded by the top brass as unwelcome to the Navy. I've forgotten now what the row was all about but his socialistic attitude on this occasion did not go down very well.

It was also claimed in the first issue: 'No newspaper in the world prints so far from its readers. Most of the time you will be four thousand miles away from the presses of *Pacific Post*'. Elaborate preparations were made for its distribution. The papers were flown out from Sydney daily, the majority going to Manus in the Admiralty Islands, an island enjoying the unenviable reputation of being 'a suffocating hole'. Here the Fleet Train was based and ships of the fighting fleet were repaired and replenished. Ships of the Fleet Train and destroyers then acted as 'news boys' delivering papers to the Fleet.

Barely seventeen days after the first issue of *Pacific Post*, the first atomic bomb was dropped on Hiroshima (6 August 1945), to be followed three days later by the Nagasaki bomb. On 14 August Japan surrendered, and for the first time in six years the Royal Navy's guns fell silent. Not so, at least for the next three months, the presses of *Pacific Post*. Eventually, however, on 10 November 1945 the last issue appeared. Its leader explained the paper's demise:

> It has been edited, printed and published in Sydney, until now the main base of the British Pacific Fleet. Victory over Japan has meant a progressive movement of ships and men from Australia to Hong Kong and Singapore... Singapore is nearly 4,000 miles from our presses, Hong Kong even further. It has been taking us an average of five days by air to bring you your *Pacific Post*.

The Fleet and other British units in the Pacific would now receive their home and sports news from *SEAC*, the daily newspaper of South East Asia Command (edited by Frank Owen of the *Evening Standard*, one of Lord Beaverbrook's protégés).

Pacific Post explained that starting on 1 December 1945 *SEAC*, 'a veteran in the Forces' newspapers field before *Pacific Post* was born', would be published in Singapore, and would reach the Fleet within twenty-four hours of its leaving the presses. The leader explained:

> And so *Pacific Post* dies because *SEAC* can bring you the news from home with a minimum of delay. Over to you, *SEAC*.

It was not until mid-December 1945 that Messrs Eyles and Newton left for England on the *Aquitania*, (where a ship's paper, the *Aqua-Daily* was produced). Mr Eyles carried on in Fleet Street journalism, while Mr Newton worked, until retirement, with the Admiralty's Public Relations branch.

Looking back after nearly fifty years, Mr Eyles reflected on the short but successful life of the *Pacific Post*:

> I think the paper certainly achieved its object of keeping ships' companies in touch with home and world news, and helped to make them rather less 'bolshie' about a separation

from England that threatened to last a long time, and plunge them into great danger. Many of these men had already experienced five hard years of war in other spheres, and a lot of them were 'hostilities only' ratings who were itching to get back to civilian life.

For, as the first issue put it:

Rarely is the birth of a newspaper conceived in such a spirit of altruism as is the *Pacific Post*. No advertiser and no shareholder is responsible for its appearance on your mess decks and in your wardrooms. It is your paper.

Notes

1. Stephen W Roskill, *The War at Sea 1939-1945*, Vol. III Part 2, HMSO, London, 1961, p 202.
2. Combined Chiefs of Staff Report to Roosevelt and Churchill, 16 September 1944, quoted in Samuel E Morison, *History of United States Naval Operations in World War II, Vol. XIV*, Little Brown, Boston, 1968, p 103.
3. Richard Humble, *Fraser of North Cape*, Routledge & Kegan Paul, London, 1983, p 257.
4. Admiral Sir Arthur J Power, 'The carrier-borne aircraft attacks on oil refineries in the Palembang (Sumatra) area in January 1945', Supplement to *London Gazette*, 3 April 1951, pp 1806 - 1808.
5. Morison op cit, pp 382 - 388. The US Navy used a more highly structural approach to the designation of naval units than did their British allies. 5 indicated 5th Fleet, 7 the 7th Task Force within that Fleet. Sub-components of Task Forces, called Task Groups, were indicated by adding a number after a decimal point, as in turn were sub-components of Task Groups, called Task Units. While TF57 had twenty-two ships, Mitscher's TF58 had eighty-eight.
6. Admiral Sir Bruce A Fraser, 'The contribution of the British Pacific Fleet to the assault on Okinawa, 1945', supplement to *London Gazette*, 1 June 1948, p 3294.
7. John Winton, *The Forgotten Fleet*, Coward-McCann, New York, 1970, p 122.
8. Morison, op cit, p 250. Spruance had lost the carrier *Hancock*, crippled on 7 April, and a second carrier, *Intrepid*, on 16 April.
9. Winton, op cit, p 135.
10. A *Formidable Commission*, Seeley Service, London, 1947, pp 75-81.
11. Fraser, op cit, pp 3307-3308.
12. Roskill, op cit, p 190. By June 1944, the size of the US Pacific Fleet had led to two officers being appointed under Nimitz to co-ordinate alternate assaults. When Admiral Ray Spruance was at sea the fleet was termed the 5th Fleet, and when he handed over to Admiral W F Halsey it became the 3rd.
13. Roskill, op cit, pp 362-363.
14. William F Halsey & J Bryan, *Admiral Halsey's Story*, McGraw-Hill, New York, 1947, pp 261-262.
15. V E Tarrant, *King George V Class Battleships*, Arms & Armour, London, 1991, p 250.
16. Admiralty, *The War at Sea, September 1939 - September 1945: Preliminary Narrative*, Vol. VI, Admiralty Technical and Staff Duties Division, London, 1945, p 46.

Further Reading

Stuart Eadon, *Kamikaze*, Square One Publications, Worcester, 1991 (anecdotal material).
Edwyn Gray, *Operation Pacific*, Naval Institute Press, Annapolis, 1989.
Peter C Smith, *Task Force 57*, William Kimber, London, 1969 (like Gray's book, an operational history).
Philip Vian, *Action This Day*, Frederick Muller, London, 1960 (Vian's autobiography).
Pacific Post (a full run of which is held by the Department of Printed Books).

Acknowledgements

The Department of Printed Books is most grateful to Mr Frank Eyles and the late Mr Don Newton for their help and co-operation in the preparation of this article. Special thanks go to Mr Newton, who generously donated to the Imperial War Museum a complete run of the *Pacific Post* in 1991.

'When d'you scarper? When d'you go into action? That's the nightmare.' The destruction of the South Nottinghamshire Hussars at Knightsbridge, 27 May - 6 June 1942

Peter Hart

Peter Hart is an interviewer with the Department of Sound Records.

Just over fifty years ago a territorial unit of artillery was caught in the Western Desert by an overwhelming concentration of German tanks and motorised infantry. With no British infantry and tank support of their own it was a hopeless position, but they had been ordered not to withdraw. The outcome was inevitable and this article is drawn from the reminiscences of those lucky few to survive.

The South Nottinghamshire Hussars, whose courageous part in this episode is told here, had been reorganised after the First World War as 107 Regiment, Royal Horse Artillery. Originally issued with 18-pounders dating from the First World War, by 1941 they had been armed with the ubiquitous 25-pounder gun howitzers. Colonel William Seely was in command and his unit consisted of three batteries: 425 Battery made up of A and E Troops under Major Peter Birkin; 426 Battery made up of C and F Troops under Major William Barber; and the newly-created 520 Battery made up of B and D Troops under Peter Birkin's cousin, Major Gary Birkin. This account has been written using excerpts from a series of interviews conducted by the Imperial War Museum's Department of Sound Records on the South Notts Hussars in an attempt to record for posterity an all round and detailed portrayal of life in an artillery regiment in the Second World War. The regiment was chosen for such concentrated research because of the variety and quality of the service experience which the unit faced throughout the war, coupled with the unstinting encouragement of the Regimental Association. The interviews were made in the veterans' own homes and vary in length from a modest hour and a half to an intimidating twenty-five hours! The story that has emerged will, I hope, demonstrate the value of interlocking accounts in illuminating what desert fighting was actually like for generations who have no such common points of reference.

The regiment had been mobilised in Nottingham in September 1939 and sent to Palestine to

The South Notts Hussars' acorn cap badge. H25681

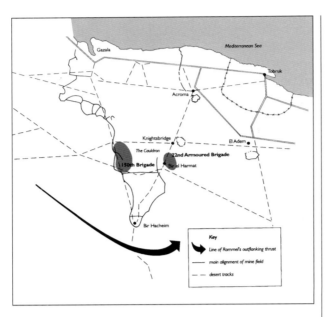

The Gazala Lines, 27 May - 6 June 1942

complete its training in January 1940. In June 1940, they were moved into the Mersa Matruh sector where they were to remain as garrison troops until December 1940. This was a period of intense boredom relieved mainly by the unwelcome attentions of Italian high-level bombers which provided the gunners with their first experience under fire. After a period in the Suez Canal area, they were moved up to Tobruk in April 1941 and played a vital role as part of the meagre artillery defences of the Tobruk garrison throughout that epic siege until Tobruk was finally relieved in December 1941. They then spent a period of much-needed rest and re-equipment in Egypt. During April and May of 1942 the regiment slowly moved up towards the front line in the Western Desert whilst endlessly practising for their mobile role as part of the 22nd Armoured Brigade with the 1st Armoured Division. As such, each battery was assigned to work with a tank regiment. Thus, 425 Battery was attached to 3rd County of London Yeomanry; 426 Battery to 4th County of London Yeomanry; and 520 Battery to the Royal Gloucestershire Hussars.

The Battle of Gazala, of which the South Notts Hussars' last stand forms just a small part, was a confusing series of engagements which resulted from the almost simultaneous attempts by the British and Axis forces to launch offensives in the Gazala sector of the Western Desert in late May 1942. In the lull that followed the success of Operation 'Crusader' in raising the siege of Tobruk, the British Eighth Army under General Claude

Auchinleck had developed a fixed defensive line behind which its armoured units would be reorganised in preparation for a further offensive. This line consisted of a series of self-contained all round defensive positions, or 'boxes', linked by minefields which stretched from the Mediterranean coast to Bir Hacheim (see map). Unfortunately, the left flank exposed south of Bir Hacheim gave an ideal opportunity for manoeuvre to General Erwin Rommel's Afrika Korps and he was the first to strike. In order to pin the British reserves in the north, he feigned a major attack in the coastal area throughout 26 May, while that same night a highly mobile force consisting of the Italian XXth Corps, the 90th Light Division and the 21st and 15th Panzer Divisions swept round the south of the Bir Hacheim minefield to fall on the vulnerable British southern flank early on 27 May.

On the night of 26 May the South Notts Hussars were ignorant of any approaching danger. At dusk, 425 and 426 Batteries were close to the junction of two desert tracks known as Knightsbridge, while 520 Battery was well to the south, in front of the gap in the minefield, at Bir el Harmat. Driver Richard Hutton, for one, was completely at ease with the situation they were in:

> The Colonel came round and I heard him telling everybody, 'We're having a very early move in the morning so nobody need dig in..' Well, that suited me - I wasn't very fond of digging. I was very pleased. [1]

Of course, although the guns and vehicles were not being dug in, any desert veterans worth their salt would always dig slit trenches for their own protection before they settled in for the night. Second Lieutenant Herbert Bonnello, who had served in the ranks with the regiment before his promotion, was equally unaware of the danger posed by the approach of Rommel's right hook round the British defences:

> The guns were pointing westwards over the minefield. All the supporting trucks were in line, dispersed at the back. I noticed as I was getting ready to get down in the old sleeping bag there was a tremendous amount of activity by flares on the other side of the minefield. No-one realised the import of these flares. Nobody had the slightest idea of what was coming. I can remember we kicked a football about that particular night. [2]

Members of the South Notts Hussars in relaxed mood. AUS 917

For Sergeant Harold Harper too it seemed to be just another night in the desert with no particular cause for alarm:

> Sergeant Major Earnshaw, the Battery Sergeant Major, and myself went across to one of the B Troop positions and sat in the back of a 15 hundredweight truck and under the direction of Sergeant Bland were taught the elements of contract bridge by the help of a hurricane lamp. When we left just after midnight and wound our way across the moonlit desert you could have heard a pin drop. [3]

On awakening, the situation still seemed normal and when, after breakfast, Harper and his comrades spotted a dust cloud on the horizon, they paid no attention, presuming it to be some of their own troops on manoeuvres. [4]

The first sign that trouble was brewing came in a telephone call from Regimental Headquarters announcing that the Germans were very close and seemingly moving down from the south. The 520 Battery commander, Major Gary Birkin and his brother, Captain Ivor Birkin, in command of D Troop, went out to investigate in two of the armoured cars used as mobile observation posts. They were en route to the Royal Gloucestershire Hussars' Regimental Headquarters when they ran right into the German tanks sweeping round the Bir Hacheim minefield. Harper was in Ivor Birkin's armoured car acting as his observation post assistant. He described what happened next:

We had only gone about six or seven hundred yards when we heard a gabbling version on the battery commander's radio which immediately told us something was wrong. Captain Birkin jumped out and dashed across, fifty to sixty yards. I followed him. When we reached the truck - I've never seen anything like it in my life. Major Birkin lay flat on the floor, obviously dead. I went to the back and opened up the two doors at the back of the armoured car. Apparently the armour-piercing shell had gone clear through the middle of the battery commander as he was standing up and chopped off the heads of the two radio operators. All you could see was these two lads, their hands still holding their mouthpieces, although their heads were lying on the floor. The third radio operator was the one gabbling the message. He jumped out of the truck. My biggest problem was to persuade Birkin to leave his brother. There was a little more than a couple of officers involved here. I said, 'Come along, you must come back'. He said, 'No, you get back. I'll see what I can do'. And he ordered me back to our original armoured car. [5]

Although he obeyed the direct order, Harper decided he must try to pick up Ivor Birkin. As the armoured car manoeuvred round:

> Just out of a cloud of sand came a Royal Gloucester Hussars' Grant tank. We hit it head on and we literally bounced back, five or six yards. The next thing we saw the engine was on fire, so we all had to jump out. In the meantime we had also accidentally run over the laddie, who was the only one left from Major Birkin's crew, so we had to drag him with us as we dashed across and told Captain Birkin what had happened. There we were, stranded. [6] *Harold Harper*

They managed to board the only remaining functioning British tank in the locality. Harper concludes this part of the story:

> We all jumped on the back of a tank of the County of London Yeomanry and lay flat. The tank commander had no idea that we were there and kept firing. We had to keep

Close up of 25-pounder field howitzer in action in Knightsbridge area. E12711

dodging as best we could when the turret and barrel kept swinging round. One of our fellows fell off and we thought he'd been crushed to death. Most of us received wounds of some description from the German shelling, although at the time we weren't aware of their extent - there was too much happening. [7]

Eventually, the tank commander heard them and took them back to the 520 Battery wagon lines for medical treatment. The wounded, including Harper who had crushed ribs and shrapnel in his knee, were then taken to the field dressing station.

Unfortunately, neither of the OP cars had managed to get off a warning radio message to the South Notts Hussars. Back at the 520 Battery position, Hutton attended to one of life's necessities in the vicinity of the wagon lines:

I'd made myself a permanent lavatory seat out of a petrol tin - all cut with a pear-shaped hole. I took that and a spade, dug myself a little hole, put this seat on top of it and I sat on it reading some magazine. I was sitting there and in the sand around me there were bits of stuff flying up all round me. 'What the bloody hell's that?' I couldn't hear any bangs or whistles, but it was like somebody was bloody well shooting at me. I could see a tank way back on the horizon - I presumed it was one of ours practising and had not seen me. I smartly pulled my trousers up and all of a sudden one of the new officers came rushing up and said we need every spare man to help dig the guns in. [8]

At the 520 Battery gun positions there was chaos:

30

We were trying to find what was going on with the radio, standing by the side of the pick-up truck. As far as B Troop were concerned it seemed to happen so quickly that we were more flabbergasted than panicked. B Troop had to turn round and face the other direction, D Troop were able to go, they were on the other side of all this line of vehicles and that shielded them and they managed to get their gun towers, limber up and push off. We were in the middle in a slit trench under fire. I should have gone. Clearly the attack was coming from the south and it was too late to go back towards Cairo, you had to go north. We should have gone much sooner. When do you scarper, when do you go into action? That was the biggest worry, that's the biggest nightmare. [9] *Herbert Bonnello*

Scores of German tanks swirled up to B Troop. One incident remained vividly in Bonnello's mind:

> I had a close picture of Sergeant Taylor's gun action. It was an amazing thing. He did an open sight action all on his own. I think most of his chaps had been killed. He hit this tank at fifty yards and it was just like a knife going through butter. The turret came straight off and bounced at the back. [10]

Sergeant Taylor was to receive the DCM. Bonnello had been forced to take cover in a slit trench and the situation was now utterly hopeless:

> If tank crew see enemy in a slit trench they can crush you - that was a big worry. I saw this big tank coming and it just missed us. Eventually the position was completely overrun. The tank crew captured us. [11]

The tanks swept in from the south and Hutton, ensconced in the wagon lines, was forced to take cover:

> There I was, all by myself. I could hear this squeaking, creaking noises that tanks make. I bobbed my head up and soon put it down again - they'd got dirty big black crosses on! Three German tanks all within spitting distance. Our guns are shooting at these tanks and they're shooting at our guns. All bloody hell was let loose. There's a hell of a

difference from being in action with one of your pals so that you can make silly jokes about it, but when you're on your own it's a different cup of tea altogether. [12]

Two of the tanks moved forward to overrun the gun position and German infantry appeared:

> I saw chaps walking about with their hands up so I came out with my hands up. It wasn't long before your arms begin to ache! [13] *Bill Hutton*

Although D Troop escaped this debacle with few casualties, B Troop ceased to exist as a fighting unit. To the north, nearer the Knightsbridge junction, 425 Battery started the day facing west on a minefield some two miles to the south west of Knightsbridge. Gun Sergeant John Walker, in charge of Number 1 gun in E Troop, had been a pre-war territorial and, as an enthusiastic soldier, hoped to be sent to be trained as an officer. His first inkling of the attack on 520 Battery came from under his feet:

> We felt the ground shaking which we knew from experience was either artillery or dive bombers. We immediately went to our guns and we could then see smoke on the horizon and we knew there was a battle. [14]

Lance-Sergeant Ted Whittaker, whose artistic talents had produced a number of cartoons satirising army life in the desert, was the signaller in the armoured car of Major Peter Birkin, commander of 425 Battery, and the cousin of Gary and Ivor Birkin:

> Major Birkin got all the information he could and said, 'We'd better go to see what's happened to 520', as we were about the nearest. We were very apprehensive: this is the complete unknown, this was mobile warfare. We simply went towards the noise. Before we got far we met Captain Shakespear in his truck, coming back in a tearing hurry. We stopped and he shouted across, he was absolutely hopping mad. [15]

Shakespear explained the situation and said, '"The bastards have killed Gary". Peter said, "Oh my God, are you sure?" He said, "Absolutely".' Meanwhile 425 Battery moved a little to the east immediately alongside the Knightsbridge box and alongside the remaining D Troop of 520 Battery. Not long after, German tanks made a concerted effort to break through from the south. For John Walker and his gun team it was a tense period:

> Willie Pringle, our Captain, walked along and said, 'Under no circumstances must you fire until you are given an order.' The heat haze slowly dissolved into physical things. On the horizon you saw a vehicle which looked like a shadow and the heat haze made it jump up and down and it slowly became a vehicle or tank. Our Sergeant Major, George Attewell, walked round and asked if we were alright. We just lay there until they started to shoot at us. We were under a hail of machine gun bullets and lost fairly quickly the layer on the next gun to me and one of my team got a bullet through his leg. We were frightfully lucky. [16]

Not everyone in the gun teams appreciated the tactic of holding fire until the enemy were so close:

> We'd got a round up the spout ready. We'd been told to load but not to fire until they came in close - until we could see the whites of their eyes. Daft! We had to just sit there. I remember this Irish gun layer said, 'I wish they'd let us fire, I've got two in me sights'. We were firing from open sights when we started - if you hit him it's alright - but meantime he's firing at you with his gun, machine-gunning you at the same time and also twisting and turning, zig-zagging towards you. We got one or two shots off when this one hit us. It dropped just underneath the gun shield, as far as I know. I was on the left hand side of the gun where you load up with your right hand, crouched down, me head right under the gun layer's seat with this 25-pounder round ready to load up again. Me arm went all dead, it was just like old rope, just hanging all sort of any road. You could see the bones through me flesh. [17] *Ted Holmes*

Walker had also opened fire on the tanks:

> We didn't shoot until they were well within range, you could identify them and train your gun on a particular tank. We all opened fire at the same moment at little more than two thousand yards. We were firing cap on HE - it

hit and exploded a fraction later - the idea being that it would blow up inside the tank rather than outside. The first one that we hit - the whole tank went red - my layer, Frank Bush, threw his hat in the air. Willie Pringle said in his Scotch accent, 'Never mind that, get another one!' [18]

Major Peter Birkin and his crew spent the day liaising with the tanks of 3rd County of London Yeomanry, organising support fire for them from the battery. Whittaker thus found himself right in the middle of a tank battle with shrapnel and bullets flying all around them. Then, right in the middle of this action, the regimental history refers to a dramatic incident. 'One of the tyres on the exposed side of Major Birkin's armoured car had been punctured by a machine gun bullet. Though the car drew intense enemy fire, Gunner Worley coolly changed the wheel under a hail of small arms fire.'[19] Whittaker gives his own - rather more colourful - account of the incident:

> All of a sudden the car started to lurch. David Worley said something gentle like, 'What the f****** hell's happened to us?' We hopped out and we'd got a puncture – front wheel. You can imagine! The tanks were at fairly long range, but by this time they'd come over the hill and there was quite a bunch of them. We couldn't get the spare wheel off. I don't know whether it was just because we were terrified or whether the nuts were tight. Talk about fingers and thumbs! We finally got the spare wheel off. The jacking up an armoured car - it's heavy - we were frantic. We got this ruddy wheel off. We put two wheel bolts on and Dave said, 'What do you reckon?' I said, 'Get in the bloody car!' We hopped in, the major said, 'OK?' and off we went. [20] *Ted Whittaker*

They found that night that they'd cross threaded both nuts! 'That's what they called "Coolly changed the wheel under fire!"' [21]

The German tanks fell back and 425 Battery, with its supporting tank regiment, had played a considerable role in preventing a complete German breakthrough. Further to the north, 426 Battery was in action all day in support of its tank regiment and also had a reasonably successful day.

The stiff resistance offered by the South Notts Hussars and their fellow units in the Knightsbridge area meant that Rommel's plan had not been as successful as he would have wished. Although he had penetrated deep behind the British positions as a result of his sweep round the Bir Hacheim minefield, it was at the cost of a third of his tanks, and others were immobilised due to shortages of fuel. At this stage, all such supplies had to travel right round the British minefields in order to reach his advanced forces. Rommel persisted with his attempts to break through to the north behind the British lines until 29 May, but by then his communication and supply situation was so critical that he resolved to turn back to the west and smash through the British minefields guarded by the 150th Brigade 'box'. If this could be achieved, it would serve the dual purpose of providing a greatly shortened supply route and, of course, a means of escape back to his own lines should such a course of action become necessary. After severe fighting, the 150th box was overrun on 1 June and Rommel had thus secured his direct route through to his forces, which were then concentrated in the area known as the Cauldron, west of the Knightsbridge junction. In the confusion, the British generals were unaware of this development and it seemed to them that Rommel had been beaten back. Although intelligence reports warned that the Germans were building up their strength in the Cauldron, they were considered mistaken and consequently a small general advance was ordered into the Cauldron on 5 June in order to capitalise on the imagined success.

The plan was for the 10th Indian Brigade of the 5th Indian Division to move westwards, after a heavy preliminary artillery bombardment, to drive a wedge through the German anti-tank screen. Once this had been achieved the augmented 7th Armoured Division would then follow up through the gap created to destroy the German forces in the Cauldron.

Since 1 June the South Notts Hussars had been in a position north-east of the Knightsbridge junction in company with the 7th Armoured Brigade and the 11th Royal Horse Artillery. The men shared the optimism of their generals. 'The impression we got was that we had almost won it and that we were going to go forward, that we were chasing them.' [22] During 4 June the specialists were kept busy preparing the fire programme to support the advance of the 10th Indian Infantry Brigade. Once this had been carried out the unit was to return to the control of the 22nd Armoured Brigade for the advance into the Cauldron.

The artillery barrage started at 03.30 and on its completion the South Notts Hussars moved forward to take up what was to be their final resting place in a hollow in the Cauldron. Gun Sergeant Ray Ellis of A Troop was

The sign marking the Knightsbridge junction of two desert tracks. E12690

soon aware of the mistake the British generals had made in deciding that Rommel was retreating:

> As we topped the rise, it was as if the sky had exploded all around us. The German had been wise to our intentions, and had quietly withdrawn his forces beyond the other edge of the depression. Our barrage had been fired into empty ground, and had been to no avail at all. Now he was ready and waiting for us and we ran straight into a hail of deadly accurate fire. [23]

The seriousness of the situation was obvious:

> It was a little bit like a saucer, sloping upwards from the centre. We were put in position on a very exposed piece of ground with the enemy in front of us where they could see us better than we could see them. They had the opportunity of coming round both of our flanks underneath the lips of the saucer. From the moment we dug ourselves in as best we could, it never felt like a happy place to be. [24]
> *John Walker*

Any differences between the ranks tended to evaporate in such moments:

I can remember when we were moving into our last stand, my officer was stood up with his head poking out. He said to me, 'Are you frightened?' I says, 'I am!', because there were shells bursting all over the place. He says, 'Yes and so am I!' [25] *Harold Thompson*

To the left of 425 Battery was the surviving D Troop of 520 Battery whilst 426 Battery was to the right and slightly in front. The battle began in earnest:

On 5 June we had a major attack on us which culminated in the evening in them taking up positions almost on our doorstep. Although they didn't overrun us they were able to stay where they were instead of withdrawing, finding protected positions for their tanks. I remember shooting with a rifle at Germans digging in. It was a very unpleasant sensation having a rest on the evening of the 5th knowing that they were going to start an attack. Most of us actually went to sleep and, this might sound very far fetched, but I put my pyjamas on! But I don't think anybody had more than an hour or so's sleep. It wouldn't be until about eleven when things were quiet and we were ready and at our posts by three in the morning. [26] *John Walker*

As the infantry of the 10th Indian Brigade had been driven back, the South Notts Hussars were almost totally exposed to attack from both German tanks and infantry when dawn broke on 6 June:

During the night they told us not to be alarmed: the British tanks were going out to re-fuel and re-arm. On 6 June we stood to from before first light. As it got light we looked up the ridge and there were the tanks in position - we could just see the tops of them silhouetted. As it got a bit lighter we knew we were for it – they were German tanks, hull down. [27] *Ted Whittaker*

There were clear signs of impending disaster:

The Stukas came over and I looked out and there was purple smoke all round us. That was the identification system for the Jerries. It showed them where their positions were and we were completely surrounded. [28] *Jack Sykes*

25-pounder field howitzer in action in Knightsbridge area. E12708

Despite this the orders remained the same:

Captain Slinn told me that it was true: we had been left to hold the line. He said that we had been ordered, 'to fight to the last man and the last round' and that there was to be no retreat for us. He warned me that it was going to be absolute carnage and that few of us would live to see the end of the day. [29] *Ray Ellis*

The fighting recommenced early on 6 June:

The infantry laid low and we carried on shooting where appropriate, but the tanks didn't come forward so fast on the immediate front. But there was the roar of the tank engines coming up the sides. It was a much more confused battle than the 27th. It was very confused, fast: we were shooting like mad. I remember shooting at both lorried infantry and tanks. We still never got hit ourselves, not even by a machine-gun bullet, and yet they were spurting along near us all the time. [30] *John Walker*

Walker had been fortunate, for one by one the gun crews were hit and put out of action:

We had just made a direct hit on a Mark IV tank when the whole world exploded around me. I felt myself being propelled into the air and then I hit the ground with a thud. I was dazed and my ears were ringing as I tried to stagger to my feet... When I looked round I could see that my gun was upside down and that the bodies of my gun crew were draped around it. I thought that I must be wounded, but I couldn't feel anything. My whole body was black with the blast and my arms and legs were bleeding. My shirt was torn and covered with blood. I wasn't afraid, more surprised than anything, and certainly not thinking clearly because I remained there on my knees just shaking my head. [31] *Ray Ellis*

In such a chaotic situation many of the more specialised members of the batteries found that they had little to do. Thus Signal Sergeant Fred Langford found that, 'There were very few people to communicate with so I was nearly redundant. I just tried to help wherever help was necessary. If people were trying to move a gun, lugging ammunition about.' [32] Similarly Whittaker found himself almost useless as the regiment struggled to survive:

> What use a forward observation expert is when the enemy is on your position - it's like the proverbial spare at the wedding. I've never felt so helpless. I had a word with my mates, told them what the Colonel had said - 'We've only got to hang on twelve hours' - and the reply to that was, 'A fat lot of f****** use that's going to be! [33] *Ted Whittaker*

One person who was kept busy was the regimental medical officer and so was his medical orderly, another regimental character, Harry Day:

> We set up a regimental aid post in and around a three tonner truck with canvas covering in a shallow depression. Inside the truck were four stretchers. In the space of half an hour we had thirty casualties or more and as the morning went on the casualties grew. [34] *Harry Day*

All this had to be carried out under shell fire:

> One of the wounded in the truck had a compound fracture of the humerus. The doctor was replacing the splint and the man's head was resting on my thigh as I was kneeling on the floor of the truck. An armoured piercing shell came straight

through the truck and took the man's head completely off. I rolled over with the near miss and my shorts were covered with his blood. [35] *Harry Day*

Shells constantly burst all around the South Notts Hussars' position and it seemed only a matter of time before everyone received a wound of some description:

> You could see clouds of dust and flashes. I received a leg wound from shrapnel or rock splinters - we were on hard ground. I was lying beside the pick-up. Albert Parker rolled me into a slit trench and applied a field dressing. [36] *Signal Lance-Bombardier Frank Knowles*

As casualties mounted Whittaker realised the grim extent of their losses. 'I began to realise that these were my friends, people I knew....' [37]. Signal Sergeant Jack Sykes was in an armoured car:

> I was sitting there passing messages when all of a sudden there was a bloody great bang. It filled with cordite and smoke. I remember Walter shouting, 'Jack! Jack!'. I was pretty well half unconscious because the shell had hit underneath my seat and I got the blast of it. I was wounded in my arms, back and knee. I remember he dragged me out and put me at the bottom of the slit trench. After that I took no further part in it. [38] *Jack Sykes*

The German tanks came ever closer to the position:

> Three tanks appeared around the escarpment. Dr MacFarland said, 'Harry, we're saved. Its the Gloucester Hussars!'. I said, 'Sir, the Gloucester Hussars don't have white crosses on them!' [39] *Harry Day*

Last ditch resistance continued and as gun teams were knocked out scratch teams formed to try and keep the guns firing:

> I heard Major Daniels shouting, 'Are there some gunners? I've got a 25 pounder here - somebody man it.' I thought, 'I can't sit here'. I jumped up and said, 'Here, Sir!' and there were two other fellows. He said, 'There's a few rounds in there; you might as well fire them.' Then off he drove. There was this German tank a few hundred yards away. I guessed the

range. There were three rounds, no armour piercing. We loaded this HE and fired and it went over the top of this tank. The turret turned and WHHUMP. To my horror I was the only one standing. The machine gun bullets had gone straight through the gun shield. [40] *Ted Whittaker*

Ellis, who had recovered from being blown up, made his way over to a crewless gun:

The trouble was there was no gunners left. Thank God the old spirit prevailed and they came without bidding: drivers, signallers, specialists, cooks and orderlies, they crawled forward to offer their help in manning the gun. These men had little experience in gunnery but so long as there was one gunner present to show them what to do it was possible to keep the guns in action. [41]

It was a brave move but they had run out of armour piercing shells and with hindsight many of the survivors now feel that the South Notts Hussars' resistance continued longer than was strictly necessary and that many lives were lost in the final moments to achieve very little:

There was ammunition exploding, gun limbers and ammunition trucks blowing up. Flames, smoke, horrible stink of gun powder. I went up to E Troop, I thought I might as well be with my pals. Major Daniels drove up and shouted, 'Form British square, go and form up on 426 Battery'. They were over to our right. The gunners went to hook the guns in and I went to get on the limber of the first gun in the troop. There were two or three chaps sitting on the limber. The nearest one, Harrison, was a Derby County footballer. They told me to 'F' off. The truck was moving and I put one foot in the foot rest, so I was hanging on the side of the door. We went a few yards and there was the most horrible explosion, the most enormous crash - it brought us to a standstill. There was some awful moans and it was a terrible sight: this shell had hit these blokes and this poor Harrison was practically in half.... I dropped off the door and threw myself flat. The driver Stevenson, had got half out of the door and the next armour-piercing

shell came straight through the driving cab and he was left hanging over the door. I was absolutely horrified at what had happened to these people I had been talking to only minutes before. I felt I could have sat down and cried. [42] *Ted Whittaker*

At this point Walker can have been only a few feet away from Whittaker:

Our Second in Command Major Daniels drove on the position in a staff car and he told us to pull our guns out and form 'a hollow British square'. He immediately pushed off - he didn't stay there to organise it. I was able to pull my gun out, my driver came up with the vehicle, I hitched in and we started to climb into the vehicle when a shell came right through my driver and the front of the vehicle. The vehicle was wrecked and my driver was killed and we decided that was enough. There was nothing we could do. The German tank was about fifteen yards away, no more. Other guns on the same site had already surrendered and they were just driving through us. [43]

Most of the guns were knocked out by this time and Ellis believes his was the last in action:

There was a man helping me who was a complete stranger. Our rate of fire was very slow, but we were still managing to engage the tanks who were almost upon us. Then I heard a loud rattle of a machine-gun which appeared to be almost in my ears and the man was reduced to a bloody mass as he was hurled spinning into the gun shield. I turned to see a Mark IV tank only a few yards behind us, his machine gun still aimed and smoking. I tensed myself but he held his fire. It was over and for the first time in thirteen hours the sound of gunfire ceased. [44]

Surrender had become almost inevitable. The tanks rolled all over the position:

A big clank, clank, clank right on the side of me and a German tank stopped. A German officer, with his cap on and earphone, leaned out and said, 'Where are you going?' I looked at him and made the classic remark, 'With you!'. 'Hop up', he said, 'for you the war is over!' [45] *Ted Whittaker*

Sykes lay wounded in a slit trench. 'The next thing I looked up and there was this German officer looking and they dragged me out. He said, "For you the war is over!"' [46] John Walker and his gun crew tried to get away into the desert:

> I told my men to take what they could - greatcoat, water bottle, anything they could grab. The firing had ceased. We lay down and the tank that was closest moved past and probably assumed we were dead. We lay down for no more than a minute, then we slowly edged away, walked backwards almost until we were a hundred yards away. The machine-guns on the tanks were hustling men into groups but we moved away east. We started to walk in a proper sense, looking for a vehicle. There were four of us. We got away for an hour and a half and we got out of sight. A German scout car came along, they must have just spotted movement, three men jumped out with guns and said '*Hande Hoch*!' We put our hands up. They took our revolvers off us. One of them said in English, 'For you the war is ended!' [47] *John Walker*

The Germans had certainly learnt their script!

The captured survivors faced three years as POWs in North Africa, Italy and Germany. The South Notts Hussars were re-formed as a unit from new drafts added to the very few who escaped the carnage. As such they continued to serve with distinction throughout the war. But none of the regiment ever forgot that grim week and even now when the survivors reunite each year at the Regimental Association dinner, it is an occasion of sad remembrance as each recalls the comrades who lost their lives in Nottingham's Knightsbridge disaster.

Notes

1. Department of Sound Records, interview with Richard Hutton, 1991, SR 11957.
2. Interview with Herbert Bonnello, 1991, SR 11959.
3. Interview with Harold Harper, 1989, SR 10923.
4. Harper, ibid.
5. Harper, ibid.
6. Harper, ibid.
7. Harper, ibid.
8. Hutton interview.
9. Bonnello interview.
10. Bonnello, ibid.
11. Bonnello, ibid.
12. Hutton interview.
13. Hutton, ibid.
14. Interview with John Walker, 1990, SR 11464.
15. Interview with Ted Whittaker, 1992, SR 12409.
16. Walker interview.
17. Interview withTed Holmes, 1991, SR 11958.
18. Walker interview.
19. E Dobson, *History of the South Notts Hussars*, Heral Printing Works, London, 1948, p 124.
20. Whittaker interview.
21. Whittaker, ibid.
22. Walker interview.
23. Department of Documents, papers of Ray Ellis, PP\MCR\388.
24. Walker interview.
25. Interview with Harold Thompson, 1991, SR 12242.
26. Walker interview.
27. Whittaker interview.
28. Interview with Jack Sykes, 1991, SR 11960.
29. Ellis interview.
30. Walker interview.
31. Ellis, op cit.
32. Interview with Fred Langford, 1991, SR 12240.
33. Whittaker interview.
34. Interview with Harry Day, 1992, SR 12412.
35. Day, ibid.
36. Interview with Frank Knowles, 1990, SR 11465.
37. Whittaker interview.
38. Knowles interview.
39. Day interview.
40. Whittaker interview.
41. Ellis interview.
42. Whittaker interview.
43. Walker interview.
44. Ellis interview.
45. Whittaker interview.
46. Sykes interview.
47. Walker interview.

Further Reading

A Gilbert, *The Desert War*, 1940-1942, Sidgwick & Jackson, London, 1992.
W G F Jackson, *The North African Campaign*, 1940-1943, Batsford, 1975.
I S O Playfair, *History of the Second World War, The Mediterranean and the Middle East, Vol III*, HMSO, London, 1960.
P Warner, *Auchinleck: the lonely soldier*, Buchan & Enright, London, 1981.
The oral history archives of the Department of Sound Records are open to the public, free of charge, by appointment Monday - Friday, 10am - 4.30pm. A catalogue of the South Notts Hussars interviews can be consulted in the department.

The empty battlefield

Paul Gough

This article offers an interpretation of one of the major paintings in the Imperial War Museum's collection of First World War art - *The Menin Road* by Paul Nash. The article is in two parts: the first section examines in detail the landscape of the Western Front battlefield as it might have appeared at certain times during the war. This section concentrates on the deceptive appearance of a land that was occasionally calm but always highly dangerous. The second section looks at how artists such as Paul Nash, Edward Handley-Read and Ian Strang solved the dilemma of painting the 'empty battlefield'.

> We set out ... across the bedevilled battlefield. It is no good trying to describe the land. It is roll upon roll of rather gentle downland ... but mile after mile of it, wherever you look, is blown into holes, mostly very big deep holes, half full of water, & running into each other, & without any grass, but all raw & filthy, & littered with bits of man & bits of weapons, & ragged old sandbags, helmets, skulls, barbed wire, boots with feet in them, bombs, shells, eclats, till it looked like an ash heap put as a dressing on a kind of putrid box that was cankering the whole earth.[1]

John Masefield's powerful description of the Somme battlefield has become the enduring image of the Great War on the Western Front - an endless panorama of mud and water, a colourless land stripped of all natural features. For many, such an extreme violation of the land has come to symbolise the brutality and hopelessness of the entire war. Yet Masefield, like many other non-combatant writers and artists, saw only a destroyed and inert landscape: in fact the battlefield was always active.

To the unpractised eye, a cursory glance into the battlefield yielded little. Visiting the Western Front in 1916, the writer Reginald Farrer mounted the fire-step of a front-line trench and peered into No Man's Land:

> It seemed quite unthinkable that there was another trench over there a few yards away just like our own ... Not even the shells made that brooding watchfulness more easy to grasp: they only made it more grotesque. For everything was so paralysed in calm, so unnaturally innocent and bland and balmy.

Paul Gough is Head of Fine Art at the University of the West of England, Bristol.

You simply could not take it in. [2]

Farrer became transfixed with this image of a crowded emptiness'. In his book *The Void of War* he suggested that it was wrong to regard the 'huge, haunted solitude' of the Western Front battlefield as empty at all. 'It is more' he argued, 'full of emptiness ... an emptiness that is not really empty at all.' [3]

Farrer was, of course, staring into the battlefield during one of its quieter moods, but his radical concept - that the negative, open space of the battlefield was actually occupied, indeed saturated, with positive forms - was also shared by many other writers and artists working on other parts of the Western Front. Yet, the notion of an 'empty battlefield' was also familiar to military historians. The concept dates back to the late nineteenth century when the introduction of smokeless powder and the invention of the machine rifle and Maxim gun allowed infantry to fire from well-concealed and distant positions. The Great War continued the process of emptying the battlefield: improved detection devices such as the aerial camera, refinements in the use of camouflage and the sheer weight of artillery fire that could be bought to bear on a fixed front meant that for long stretches of time the Western Front landscape was deserted by daylight.

Nevertheless, however empty the battlefield its topography had to be studied and recorded. Artillery officer P J Campbell recalled long summer days in an observation post endlessly scanning the enemy-held country beyond:

> I learnt the names of every wood and all the villages, I knew the contours of the hills and the shapes of the lakes in the valley. To see so much and to see nothing. We might have been the only men alive, my two signallers and I. And yet I knew there were thousands of hidden men in front of me ... but no one moved, everyone was waiting for the safety of darkness. [4]

Over time even the barest tract of battlefield was analysed and mapped, and its daunting emptiness divided into areas of safe and unsafe ground. One of the most crucial divisions of the battlefield began at the edge of the trench parapet - behind the soldier lay the secure lines of communication, bringing supplies, rations and relief; in front of him was a perilous landscape, unknown and highly dangerous. Yet, even that hazardous environment could be divided into three distinct bands. The most distant band was a stretch of territory untouched by war, referred to often by a Biblical analogy:

> I could ... see unspoiled land beyond the Hindenburg Line, undulating hills, little woods, villages fit to live in, trees that bore leaves, a hillside without shell-holes. It was like a Promised Land. [5]

For many soldiers though, this tract would always remain out of reach, forever locked in an unattainable future.

The second lateral band was the enemy line. Deep and labyrinthine, the German trenches were regarded with suspicion and fear - 'mysterious and fascinating'[6] wrote one front-line officer - and had to be constantly monitored. Here, at least, the artist proved himself useful by helping to study and record the features of the enemy position. Using the neutral language of topographical reportage, such painters as Adrian Hill and Leon Underwood, together with a huge number of trained engineer and artillery officers, made painstaking studies of every part of the enemy line. This was a dangerous and thankless task: getting a decent viewpoint was often impossible and, because the enemy line changed its appearance regularly, drawings had a limited use. Nevertheless, trench drawings were invaluable for developing a profile of the enemy line, especially when used in conjunction with photographs taken by aerial cameras.

The third band of land on the battlefield - one rather more difficult to record accurately - was No Man's Land. Most soldiers regarded this debatable land' [7] with a mixture of extreme caution and dread fascination. Fifty years after the war, Charles Carrington was still obsessed by the strange properties of the place:

> This side of our wire everything is familiar and every man a friend; over there, beyond their wire, is the unknown, the uncanny; there are the people about whom you can accumulate scraps of irrelevant information but whose real life you can never penetrate, the people who will shoot you dead ... [8]

During four years of warfare the shape of No Man's Land changed regularly, but from a pictorial point of view it took two distinct forms - firstly, an innocent strip of grassy meadow sandwiched between the opposing lines; and secondly, a vast, awesome brown swamp more like a desert or ocean than a part of Northern Europe. The first category - the 'garden of death' [9] - was most obvious when viewed from the air:

> What a frightful state the earth was in. For miles and miles around it had the appearance of a sieve, with hundred of thousands of shell-holes; and like a beautiful green ribbon, winding away as far as the eye could see, was that wonderful yet terrible strip of ground between the lines, No Man's Land. [10]

Like an overgrown racecourse wending its way between the opposing lines, No Man's Land could, on occasions, seem quite calm, even benign. This pastoral impression would prove difficult to translate into pictorial terms but metaphorically No Man's Land was regarded by many soldiers as an unbridgeable chasm, 'visually so near' as the poet David Jones wrote, 'yet for the feet forbidden by a great gulf'. [11]

Pictorially, the second category of No Man's Land was slightly less difficult to render. The Vorticist artist and artillery officer Percy Wyndham Lewis described the battlefield as an 'epic of mud',[12] a vast panorama of brown and grey that stretched to the horizon, swallowing man, animal and machine in its glutinous mud. The great deserts of the Western Front were, in fact, phenomena of the second half of the war, the result of five months fighting on the Somme that saw 200 square miles of Picardy reduced to an 'obscene porridge', and the systematic destruction of the land during the German retreat to the Hindenburg Line in spring 1917. But in late 1917, artists and writers had to invent a quite new language of destruction to describe the awesome devastation of the Ypres Salient, when vast areas of the land were reduced to primeval swamp. As we shall see, traditional techniques such as water-colour and innovations in the use of pictorial space became key tools in the artist's search for an equivalent to this drowned landscape.

Just as the landscape of No Man's Land can be divided into two types, so might the psychological response: on the one hand there was the pragmatic realism that supremacy had to be achieved at all costs; on the other, a complex emotional reaction to the sight of such devastation - an intense, subjective response that harks back to the Romantic era and a yearning for overwhelming, spiritual experience.

The tensions between this pragmatic and emotional response gave rise to an extraordinarily complex reading of the battle landscape. The first stage in this reading came during night patrol, when soldiers had to leave the safety of their trench and explore No Man's Land. Crawling on hands and knees, covering just a few yards in an hour, combatants soon found that both space and time in No Man's Land were subject to the most ridiculous distortions - a few minutes would seem to last an hour; an enemy trench 100 yards away seemed 'a mile in the darkness'.[13] Where No Man's Land was wider, soldiers learned to avoid predictable routes, preferring instead complicated and eccentric paths not marked on conventional charts. In a letter home, officer Keith Henderson wrote of one such 'secret' path:

> Gradually you begin to track out safe routes. Don't go near the edge of – Wood, but 200 yards inside the wood, on the north side, you're pretty comfy. Don't go near the mangled remains of – village, but keep to the right of it until you get to the wrecked aeroplane, and then turn down the remains of – trench, and you probably won't get touched. [14]

Such safe routes changed daily, perhaps hourly, partly because the dominant landmarks of the battlefield were no longer the permanent features of the landscape - trees, woods, buildings - but local, transient objects such as 'the dead major' remembered by Subaltern Mellersh as being used as a signpost on one stretch of the barren battlefield. [15]

Any understanding of the nature of space and direction on the battlefield was further complicated by the strategic importance given to key points of the front line, a value often at odds with the actual scale of the place. Hill 60, for example, an important vantage point south of Ypres, had to be defended at all costs although it was no larger than the central part of Trafalgar Square. The woods and copses of Thiepval, Mametz, Trones and Delville became infamous focal points during the Battle of the Somme, earning reputations that can seem out of proportion given the vastness of the Picardy landscape.

Yet another problem to the landscape artist was the fact that interspersed between these points of concentration were tracts of land that had been somehow spared the devastation of the fighting. Artillery officer Richard Talbot Kelly wrote of his astonishment at finding a meadow of green grass amidst the desolation of the Somme battlefield and soldiers marvelled at the 'miraculous' way in which churches and roadside calvaries survived bombardment. Ironically, the few remaining landmarks of the battlefield rarely offered any refuge for the weary foot soldier. German excellence in spotting and gun-registration meant that even the

Panoramic view of the desolation of the Western Front. Q1278

smallest target on the barest tract of land could be pinpointed by enemy fire. Infantryman Stuart Dolden remembered the poor choice of 'The Lone Tree' as an assembly point for the wounded after the Battle of Loos because 'this tree was a favourite for the German artillery'. [16] Survival soon hinged on being highly sensitive to the new order of the battle landscape, a point noted by the cartoonist Bruce Bairnsfather:

> A farm was a place where you expected a shell through the wall any minute; a tree was the sort of thing the gunners took range on; a sunset indicated a quality of light in which it was unsafe to walk abroad. [17]

Increasingly wary of normal places of congregation, soldiers learned to extract every inch of tactical advantage in the seemingly featureless environment. Charles Carrington knew the value of correctly assessing 'dead' ground: 'Every bank or hedge behind which you could jump to shelter, was a feature of the landscape, to be studied or remembered.' [18]

This inversion in the customary understanding of a landscape 'feature', like so many of the unusual properties of the landscape, would have a crucial effect on the way artists rendered the empty battlefield.

> A land pock-marked by a million shell-holes, wherein it was impossible ever to walk straight, each track or path twisting endlessly between these great sores, and in the silver mists the many battered trees of the Salient seemed to belong to a dark primitive age. [19]

This, wrote the amateur artist and artillery officer Richard

Talbot Kelly, was 'my first and last memory' of the Ypres Salient. For most artists and photographers sent to work on the Western Front, the first sight of the ravaged land was a similarly traumatic moment. Society artist and Royal Academician Sir William Orpen saw the Somme battlefield as 'mud, nothing but water, shell-holes and mud - the most gloomy, dreary abomination of desolation the mind could imagine.' [20] Working as an Official War Artist, he was mocked by one infantry officer when he expressed a wish to 'paint the Somme'. 'I could do it from memory,' said the officer, 'just a flat horizon-line and mud holes and water.' [21] Another war artist, John Singer Sargent, complained of the difficulties of finding subjects:

> The further forward one goes the more scattered and meagre everything is. The nearer to danger, the fewer and more hidden the men - the more dramatic the situation the more it becomes an empty landscape. [22]

Other artists turned this predicament to their advantage. The Scottish painter David Young Cameron, commissioned to paint a large picture of the battlefield, spent some weeks travelling up and down the old front line in early 1919 but failed to find a single viewpoint that would symbolise the effects of war on the land. Faced with the sheer scale of the desolation, the absence of discernible motifs, and the unusual state of flux that existed in the drowned land, Cameron rejected the convention of a fixed view. Instead, he chose to make a composite image of the Ypres Salient, collaged together from many impressions of the front. 'It is', he wrote 'not a portrait of any one spot (photographers can do that) but is founded on my sketches on the road from Ypres to Menin - really the road to the front.' [23]

Above: David Young Cameron, *The Battlefield of Ypres*, oil, canvas, 72" x 125", Department of Art, 2626.

Below: Paul Nash, *Men Marching at Night*, 1918, lithograph, 20¼" x 16½", Department of Art, 1605.

The official Australian photographer Frank Hurley would not have agreed with Cameron's assertion. He, too, grew increasingly frustrated by the inability to cram 'the war' onto a single negative. His efforts, he despaired, had been 'hopeless':

> Everything is on such a wide scale. Figures scattered, atmosphere dense with haze and smoke - shells that would simply not burst when required. All the elements of a picture were there, could they but be brought together and condensed. [24]

As Cameron had discovered, instead of having a single focal point, the battlefield was multi-focused; instead of solid earth, the terrain on some sectors was little more than a liquefied morass; instead of having a coherent and uniform spatial state, the landscape was often fractured and distorted.

One means of conveying the complex conditions of the battlefield lay in a re-appraisal of the pictorial function of roads, tracks and pathways in the landscape. Many patterns, for instance, were attracted to the image of a tree-lined road. Not only was it a symbol of

Edward Handley-Read, *Near Neuve Chapelle: A Road under Enemy Observation,* charcoal and water-colour, 18½" x 24¾", Department of Art, 808.

continental Europe, but an avenue of trees represented authority, direction and a forward dynamic that made a powerful impression on soldiers and artists:

> Our route led along one of the great poplar-lined roads of France, which run straight as a die for league after league. When the road dipped, the line of battalions stretched from horizon to horizon. [25]

The painter Paul Nash recognised how a formal avenue could convey an unambiguous sense of forward momentum. His lithograph *Marching at Night* is a wonderful evocation of concentrated energy, its directional impetus aided by an economical geometric style. Later in the war, as the formal avenues were smashed by artillery fire and smothered by war refuse, their role in war art changed. In Edward Handley-Read's charcoal sketch of an enemy road under observation, the directional pull of the stately avenue is checked by a wooden barrier: the new safer route is on the left of the picture via the entrance to a communications trench. In choosing this compositional arrangement, Handley-Read, perhaps a little clumsily, spells out the altered hierarchies of the 'empty battlefield'. The confident, assertive thrust of the stately avenue has been supplanted by a modest, weaving pathway relegated to a corner of the

composition. We can see further evidence of the altered directional priorities on the battle landscape in such pictures as Ian Strang's *The Menin Road with Tanks.* Symmetrically placed in the centre of the picture, the tree-lined road has no directional function at all - the surface is cratered and impassable and the tanks move from right to left across the battlefield, ignoring the forward thrust of the avenue completely.

For artists and writers, the avenue was a useful pictorial motif because it symbolised a formality and symmetry that had been shattered by war. The complex phenomena of the 'empty battlefield' were, however, much more difficult to describe in paint. In the main, this was due to the difficulties in representing the many sorts of space on the battlefield - the 'crowded emptiness' of the deserted landscape.

Before the First World War, the art movement Cubism had initiated a radical approach to the understanding of pictorial space. The innovations of Picasso and Braque challenged the strict logic of Renaissance perspective. Instead of an ordered method of rationalising space, the Cubists favoured fracture and dislocation. They took multiple viewpoints of objects and advocated an end to the idea of the single viewpoint dominating a picture.

Not all artists knew of, or were influenced by, the Cubist approach to space. Many painters had to find

Ian Strang, *The Menin Road: With Tanks, 1918*, pen and water-colour, 10" x 14", Department of Art, 1641.

Adrian Hill, *Road Menders*, ink and water-colour 14½" x 20¾", Department of Art, 215.

for themselves a pictorial language appropriate to the unique conditions of the Western Front. These innovations took some interesting forms. Official War Artist Adrian Hill, for example, developed a method of 'vignetting'- an artistic form that produced a circular or ovoid picture in which the image seems to emerge from a central point gradually fading away to the edges. Hill's approach may owe something to his front-line duties in the Sniping and Scouting Section of the Honourable Artillery Company when he was regularly required to crawl into No Man's Land to draw the key positions in the enemy line, a method that caused him to concentrate on a tiny fragment of the view, every other part of the picture being reduced to hazy irrelevance. David Baxter, working as Official War Artist with the Royal Army Medical Corps, radicalised his use of water-colour in an attempt to capture the diffused spatial conditions on parts of the Ypres salient in late 1917. By layering pools of heavily diluted paint onto large sheets of thick paper, Baxter

David Baxter, *A Dirty Day in Flanders*, water-colour, 15" x 22", Department of Art, 3245.

seems to have found a pictorial equivalent to the sodden state of the battlefield. With its blobs of paint, unmodulated colour and almost random points of focus, his painting *A Dirty Day in Flanders* is a remarkable evocation of the formless land.

But it was Paul Nash who managed to fuse the language of Cubism and Vorticism with a sound knowledge of the war landscape to produce some of the most powerful images of the war. Nash had served as an infantry officer in the trenches and had witnessed the battlefield in its many states. In a letter of 1917, he marvelled at the resilience of nature:

> Where I sit now in the reserve line the place is just joyous, the dandelions are bright gold over the parapet and nearby a lilac bush is breaking into bloom: in a wood passed through on our way up, a place with an evil name, pitted and pocked with shells, the trees torn to shreds, often reeking with poison gas - a most desolate ruinous place two months back, today it was vivid green: the most broken trees even had sprouted somewhere and in the midst, from the depth of the wood's bruised heart poured out the throbbing song of nightingale. [26]

Nash summarised the 'ridiculous mad incongruity' of the ever-changing landscape in his *magnum opus* of the war, *The Menin Road*, painted for the British Government during 1918-1919. At first sight, it is the customary *leitmotif* of the Western Front - shell holes, tree stumps, an endless vista of mud and water. But it is much more than an eleven feet panorama of chaos and despair. It is also a highly sophisticated reading of the spatial disjunctions and temporal dislocation that governed No Man's Land on the empty battlefield.

The canvas is divided into three territorial

bands, each with its own directional properties. The foreground, as so often in Nash's war pictures, is crammed with insurmountable obstacles - pools of water, pyramidal concrete blocks, piled debris - which frustrate any access to the road in the centre of the picture. Between the concrete blocks and the pools there is, however, a narrow strip of flat ground that comprises the sole pathway through the foreground mess. But here, instead of offering the spectator an entry point into the picture, Nash introduces a visual barrier - a single rectangular shape - that seems to prevent any further movement through the gap. Furthermore, the rectangular shape does not conform to the dominant diagonal which dictates every other line in the picture. It is out of accord, by just a few degrees, with every other angle in the picture. It rests uneasily in the general design of the painting - a deliberate compositional trick to frustrate the spectator, and a reminder of the secret language needed to decode the battle landscape.

These subtle games of pictorial movement persist into the central territorial band. The surface of the Menin Road is painted in broad sweeps of unmodulated paint, the shell holes that puncture it are spaced - like giant foot-steps in deep snow - at regular intervals, and the avenue of trees on either side lend it some lateral momentum. But again Nash deliberately confuses the directional sense - on the left of the picture sharp diagonal shadows distort the road surface, on the right several trees are placed to offset the symmetry of the avenue, debris constantly interrupts the decorative chaos of the middle band of the picture. Here, Nash seems to imply, freedom of movement is no longer guaranteed, mobility is severely controlled and progress is always hazardous and exposed.

In the third pictorial zone beyond the road, the danger is no longer latent but very real. Two soldiers take refuge from huge explosions which give off plumes of smoke that ironically mimic the forms of verdant trees. Where many artists might have drawn the battlescape as a series of parallel bands disappearing into the distance, Nash attempted a much more sophisticated and daring approach to pictorial movement. Beyond the furthest line of trees Nash drew seven water-filled ditches; each one meanders sluggishly into the distance only to stop short of the horizon. Each of the ditches invites the eye to travel into the distance, to explore the furthest reaches of the battlefield. But each ditch, in turn, fails to open up the view and ends either in the lazy curve of an ox-bow

Paul Nash, *The Menin Road*, Oil, canvas, 72" x 125", 1919, Department of Art, 2242.

lake or is abruptly blocked by some dam-like impediment.

With a masterly understanding of the peculiarities of battlefield space, Nash has condensed into one painting three types of movement: awkward, obstructed movement across the foreground, the delicately balanced lateral sweep of the road, frustrated progress into deep space in the distance.

The Menin Road is the work of an artist whose previous experience as a soldier had rendered him extremely sensitive to the territorial demarcations of the battlefield. In a single, resounding image Nash encapsulates all that was dreadful, confusing and yet endlessly fascinating in that 'phantasmagoric land' - contradictions also wonderfully captured by war poet David Jones:

> the day by day in the wasteland, the sudden violences and long stillnesses, the sharp contours and unformed voids of that mysterious existence profoundly affected the imaginations of those who suffered it. It was a place of enchantment. [27]

Notes

1. John Masefield, letter to his wife dated 12 March 1917, quoted in *John Masefield's Letters from the Front, 1915 - 1917*, editor Peter Vansittart, Constable, London, 1984.
2. Reginald Farrer, *The Void of War*, Constable, London, 1918, p 113.
3. Ibid, pp 55.
4. P J Campbell, *In the Cannon's Mouth*, Hamish Hamilton, London, 1979, pp 218 - 219.
5. Ibid, pp 261 - 62.
6. Edwin Campion Vaughan, *Some Desperate Glory: The Diary of a Young Officer 1917*, Frederick Warne, London, 1981, p 207.
7. John Masefield, op cit, letter dated 25 September 1916.
8. Charles Carrington, *Soldier From the Wars Returning*, Hutchinson, London, 1965, p 87.
9. Patrick MacGill, *The Red Horizon*, Brandon Publishers, Ireland, 1985, p 246
10. Geoffrey H Malins, *How I Filmed the War*, Herbert Jenkins, London, 1920, p 112.
11. David Jones, *In Parenthesis*, Faber and Faber, London, 1937/1978, p 66.
12. Wyndham Lewis, *Blasting and Bombardiering*, Eyre and Spottiswoode,

London, 1937, p 161.
13. Phillip Gibbs, *The Realities of War*, Heinemann, London, 1920, p 193.
14. Keith Henderson, *Letters to Helen*, 1917, p 60.
15. H E L Mellersh, *A Schoolboy into War*, William Kimber, London, 1978, p 88.
16. A Stuart Dolden, *Cannon Fodder*, Blandford Press, Poole, 1980, p 39.
17. Bruce Bairnsfather, *Bullets and Billets*, Grant Richards, London, 1916, p 238.
18. Charles Carrington, op cit, p 85.
19. R.B. Talbot Kelly, *A Subaltern's Odyssey: memoirs of the Great War 1915 - 1917*, William Kimber, London, 1980, p 63.
20. William Orpen, *An Onlooker in France*, Williams and Norgate, 1921, p 36.
21. Ibid, p 20.
22. Charles Merrill Mount, *John Singer Sargent: An Autobiography*, The Crescent Press, 1957, p 297.
23. Cameron to Yockney, 8.11.1919, Correspondence file 202/5, Department of Art, IWM.
24. Hurley's diary, quoted in Lennard Bickel, *In Search of Frank Hurley*, Macmillan, Australia, 1980, p 61.

25. Charles Douie, *The Weary Road: Recollections of a Subaltern of Infantry*, John Murray, 1929, facsimile reprint, Strong Oak Press, 1988, p 82.
26. Paul Nash, *Outline: An Autobiography and Other Writings*, Faber, 1949, p 187.
27. David Jones, op cit, p X.

Further reading

Jay Appleton, *The Experience of Landscape*, Wiley, London, 1975.
Andrew Causey, *Paul Nash*, Clarendon Press, Oxford, 1980.
Paul Fussell, *The Great War and Modern Memory*, Oxford University Press, 1975.
Paul Gough, *Painting the Landscape of Battle: the Development of Pictorial Language in British Art on the Western Front, 1914 - 1918*. unpublished PhD thesis, copy in Department of Art, IWM.
Meirion and Susie Harries, *The War Artists*, Michael Joseph in association with the Imperial War Museum and the Tate Gallery, London, 1983.
Samuel Hynes, *A War Imagined: The First World War and English Culture*,

The Bodley Head, London, 1990.
William Godfrey Newton, *Military Landscape and Target Indication*, Hugh Rees Ltd, London, 1915.
LC Peltier and GE Pearcy, *Military Geography*, Van Nostrand, Princeton, USA, 1986.

Acknowledgements:

Thanks are due to Angela Weight, Keeper, and to Jenny Wood, Mike Moody and Pauline Allwright in the Department of Art; to Peter Simkins and Joe Darracott for advice and encouragement; and to the Research Committee of the Faculty of Art, Media and Design at the University of the West of England, Bristol.

The war art of C R W Nevinson

Charles Doherty

Charles Doherty is Assistant
Professor of
Art History at Loyola
University, New Orleans.

The British First World War artist C R W Nevinson (1889-1946) produced approximately 170 war images in a variety of media. His innovative paintings and prints of modern warfare documented the anguish and realities of the soldier's trench life amongst machine-guns, barbed wire, and explosions in war-torn landscapes. One of the earliest of the British artists to witness the Western Front at first hand, he provided colourful records of the war for a home front eager and interested in viewing non-photographic black-and-white images of the conflict. His first representations of the war appeared in British newspapers and periodicals in early 1915, and his work was widely reproduced in the popular press thereafter, both at home and abroad throughout the war. Owing in part to the public's knowledge of his work, he was the first young modern artist chosen by the Department of Information to participate in the official war artists' scheme. Although his career would later be eclipsed by others', he was recognised in 1917 as a significant and influential artist who could aid the government's war effort. Arnold Bennett referred to Nevinson in a memo to his colleagues on the British War Memorials Committee as 'the chief war painter.'[1]

Christopher Richard Wynne Nevinson was born in Hampstead on 13 August 1889, the only son of two well-known figures in journalism and social issues: Henry Wood Nevinson (1856-1941), perhaps the most eminent British war correspondent of his generation, and Margaret Wynne Jones Nevinson (1860?- 1932), a noted writer and spokesperson for women's suffrage and social welfare concerns. She was also one of the first female Justices of the Peace in London. The Nevinsons' contacts with noted figures within the ranks of journalism, government, and the art world greatly assisted Nevinson's early rise to prominence in the art pages before and during the war.[2]

Although Nevinson received formal art training at the Slade School of Art (1908-12), he believed his travels to the Continent were more influential in his development as an artist. In 1912 he moved to Paris where contact with the flourishing avant-garde movements included associations with the Italian artists Gino Severini (1883-1966), Umberto Boccioni (1882-1916), and others known as Futurists.[3] These rebel-anarchists heralded speed, motion, and machines, while espousing the love of danger, audacity, and revolt as a means of destroying the outmoded values and institutions of the past centuries. Their more than twenty pre-war

C R W Nevinson, *Marching Men*, c.1915-16, gouache, 5½ x 8 inches,
Department of Art, 5218.

manifestos and related documents outlining the Futurist positions were largely the inspiration of their provocative impresario-leader, F T Marinetti (1876-1944). In his founding manifesto of 1909, Marinetti glorified militarism, patriotism, and war; the latter he described as 'the world's only hygiene'. His bombastic rhetoric proclaimed the desire to 'destroy the museums, libraries, academies of every kind' while celebrating 'crowds excited by work, by pleasure, and by riot'. The bustle of modern life symbolically represented by shipyards, railway stations, factories, ocean-going steamers, and aeroplanes were all artistic subjects recommended by Marinetti for his Futurist disciples. [4]

Nevinson adopted a Futurist compositional style similar to that of the pre-war Cubist artists for his motion-filled, dynamic interpretations of a machine-oriented society. Through use of bold abstract lines and fractured geometric planes of saturated colours, he produced Futurist images of London streets, of railyards with departing trains, and of people engaging in energetic activities. In June 1914, he co-authored the Futurist manifesto *Vital English Art* with Marinetti, and for much of the war would be labelled 'The English Futurist' by a bemused and sometimes scornful press. [5] In the autumn of 1914 when the extent of the German atrocities was reported in the British press, however, Nevinson privately revealed an interest in distancing himself from the Futurist movement. [6] But the press did not forget his allegiance to the rebellious group and continued to refer to him as a Futurist or former Futurist for the rest of the war.

Between 1914 and 1915, Nevinson produced one of his most Futurist series of images entitled *Returning to the Trenches*. In the gouache version, sometimes referred to as *Marching Men*, and in the oil now in the National Gallery of Canada, he used geometric red, blue, brass and steel-coloured wedges to suggest the frenzied rush of the French *poilus* to the front. [7] Their brightly-coloured uniforms, sharply-configured kits, and bayonets all in motion cleave the composition into segmented arcs and polygons. The art critic for the *Observer*, P G Konody, described the painting as, 'the most logical, the most convincing practical demonstration of Futurist principles that I have so far seen. No purely representative method could ever render so happily the swinging rhythm of the marching soldiers' movements.' [8]

Nevinson's youthful espousal of aggressive rhetoric was severely tested by his close-range viewing of the war. His 1914-15 war service as an ambulance driver and motor mechanic with the Anglo-Belgian Ambulance Service, the volunteer brigade of Quakers later called the Friends' Ambulance Service, was a significant experience to shape his artistic wartime career.

H W Nevinson oversaw the preparations for their joint enlistment in this Red Cross-related organisation in late October 1914. His journal records that his son was dressing wounds on 14 November, [9] transporting the injured and dying from the first bombardment of Ypres and the battles of the Yser front. Within ten days of his arrival his ambulance had been wrecked by a shell. Over the following ten weeks, he saw, heard and smelled the realities of the evacuation shed nicknamed 'The Shambles,' a make-shift casualty clearing station at the Dunkirk railyard.[10]

When the Friends arrived at the railyard's goods shed for their first mission a fortnight earlier, they had found more than three thousand wounded and dying French soldiers attended by only six medical assistants. [11] After the war Nevinson recalled:

> By the time I had been at the Shambles a week my former life seemed to be years away. When a month had passed I felt I had been born in a nightmare. I had seen sights so revolting that man seldom conceives them in his mind and there was no shrinking even among the more sensitive of us. We could only help, and ignore shrieks, puss, gangrene, and the disembowelled. [12]

Nevinson endured the squalor and seemingly never-ending routine of driving between the front and casualty clearing stations for less than three months. Back in London in February 1915, he was writing letters to newspaper editors and granting press interviews. Following one article, entitled 'Painter of Smells at the Front,' the artist denied that he was suffering some form of shell shock. His letter of 25 February 1915, published the next day in the *Daily Express*, corrected this assessment: 'Beyond a severe attack of rheumatism, my health is better than before the war, and I am in absolutely no way suffering from any form of nerve trouble.' The issue of Nevinson's health would resurface at different times during the war. It is known that he suffered from recurring bouts of rheumatic fever, a disease most likely contracted as a child, and easily brought on by stress and overwork. [13]

One of Nevinson's earliest war oils, *The Doctor*, portrays the theatrically-lit, straw-strewn 'Shambles' where medical personnel assist the injured. Its crude and uncomfortable conditions are amplified through use of a dislocated, diagonal composition in which the halves of two stretchers jut from the lower foreground. An attending physician unties the bloodied dressings covering the head wound of a shrieking soldier in the right-centre of the picture. Nearby, another stretcher bears a soldier less fortunate, one apparently dead given his mummified appearance with blanket and cloth. In the background, another medical attendant dresses the lower-back and pelvic wounds of an awkwardly-bent semi-nude soldier. The figure's pose may have shocked the

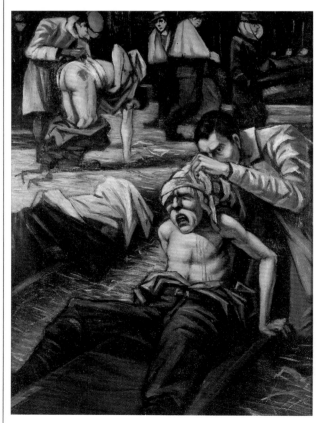

C R W Nevinson, *The Doctor*, 1916, oil on canvas, 22½ x 16 1/4 inches, Department of Art, 725.

C R W Nevinson, *La Mitrailleuse*, 1915,
oil on canvas, 24 x 20 inches, Tate Gallery 3177.
Reproduced by kind permission of the Trustees of the Tate Gallery.

home viewer now forced to confront the public humiliation to which medical treatment subjected wounded soldiers. Two of the walking wounded in the distance observe the evacuation-shed drama, drawing our attention to the pain described in the foreground. Nevinson highlights the human suffering through red accents in the foreground soldier's trousers and blood-streaked chest, and in the semi-nude soldier's open pelvic wound and the attending figure's red glove.

Unlike other early war paintings of medical settings, in which comfortable temporary hospitals were shown in converted great halls of country houses - even the chandeliered Banqueting Room of the Royal Pavilion at Brighton [14] - Nevinson describes a rough, impersonal, casualty unit near the front. His views of the medical services, including his other oil of the 'Shambles' entitled *La Patrie*, were unusual in 1915-16 in their direct, uncompromising, presentation of the casualties of modern war. Focusing on the pain and suffering of the soldiers, some with grimacing faces, bloody bandages, and open wounds, Nevinson imparts a new portrayal in British art of the realities of war.[15]

Nevinson rested in London in early 1915 while managing to paint war images from memory as well as other images of the home front. He exhibited these works in group exhibitions along with paintings like *Returning to the Trenches*. Following recovery, he joined the Royal Army Medical Corps (RAMC) and was sworn in at the Third London General Hospital (Third LGH) in Wandsworth on 1 June 1915. Nevinson Senior accompanied him for the swearing in, where he was given assurances by the attending captain that Richard would not be detailed for foreign service. [16]

Nevinson's RAMC service allowed little time for drawing and painting. His daily activities, though varied, involved arduous chores: meeting hospital trains, transporting the injured, equipping new wards, helping in the operating theatre, and building roads and repairing fences. One photograph, published in the hospital magazine, depicts Nevinson with other orderlies at work laying large logs as part of their road construction assignment. [17]

This was a strenuous period in Nevinson's life, draining him of enthusiasm for war. The regimented military way of life did not suit him: he lamented that he was able to use his head while serving in the Red Cross, whereas its use was a handicap at the Third LGH. [18] His view of hospital life was further strained by his tenure as an orderly in the psychiatry ward, which he described as 'the worst job I have ever tackled in my life.' *In the Observation Ward*, his now lost painting, depicted a portrait-like image of a drooling patient who stares vacuously at the viewer. Nevinson wrote of his service among patients living in a world of hallucination and persecution, and observed:

> I began to have an uneasy feeling that I was catching their complaint, and had it not been for the observation of one of the doctors I believe I should have become one of the barmy ones myself. Scientific or not, I am convinced that mental instability is infectious. [19]

Nevinson's health once more flagging, he was granted a leave of absence that coincided with his marriage to Kathleen Mary Knowlman, the daughter of a Welsh-speaking classicist, in Hampstead on 1 November. On the last two days of their honeymoon, he painted another significant painting of his early war years, *La Mitrailleuse*, a powerful, Futurist-inspired view of a French machine-gunner and his crew. The men and their machines are barely differentiated by colour or treatment of form: the same steel-grey tones are used for the machine and soldiers' helmets, and a slightly bluer tone for their uniforms. Seemingly oblivious to their surroundings, the three men proceed in their cold, deathly enterprise while a colleague lies slumped and dead beneath them. A faint, aqua-green pallor, which Nevinson used later in his portrayal of death, *Paths of Glory*, distinguishes the face of the dead soldier. The use of cold, metallic colours, firm outlines, and inter-connecting geometric components forcefully proclaimed another emphatic statement of war: man as deathly and sinister as his new weapon, the machine-gun. [20]

The 1916 Leicester Galleries exhibition

Nevinson never returned to active duty at the Third LGH. He was invalided out of the RAMC in January 1916 for reasons of poor health, and a period of convalescence in Hampstead allowed him to devote more time to painting and printmaking. [21] He submitted occasional war images to group exhibitions during 1916, and by May one critic conceded: 'he is distinctly "catching on." He has sold more pictures this year than ever before, three of them having been actually acquired for public galleries.' [22] The majority of Nevinson's energy was now channelled toward his first one-man show at the Leicester Galleries in September.

Previous London war art exhibitions of 1915-16, most notably at the Fine Art Society, the Goupil Galleries, and the Leicester Galleries, exhibited non-controversial works of a certain similarity: war satires,

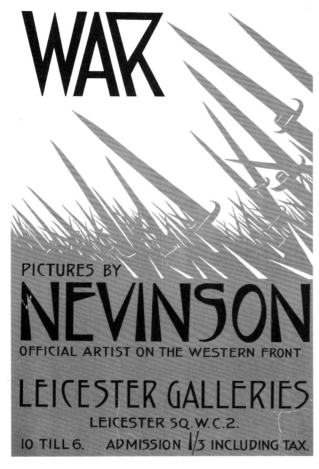

C R W Nevinson, *War Pictures by Nevinson* [Poster for Leicester Galleries exhibition, March 1918], 1917?-18, lithograph, 30 x 20 inches, Department of Art. PST 0411

the end of the year, Rutter would remember Nevinson's 1916 works as 'indisputably the most powerful, original and impressive paintings yet inspired by the European war.' [25]

At the Leicester Galleries, Nevinson demonstrated an unusual versatility and insight uncommon in a first one-man show in exhibiting strong, thought-provoking, colourful oils, and stark, confrontational, black-and-white prints. There were thirty-five paintings, eighteen drawings and etchings, and one work of sculpture, recalling his tenure as a hospital orderly (*Night Arrival of Wounded*) and as an ambulance driver (*The Doctor* and *La Patrie*). [26] His memories of the front included the oil and drypoint-etching entitled *Twilight*: it depicts a soldier carrying a wounded comrade on his back after a night battle and records the selfless dedication and devotion of the soldier to his fellow men. Nevinson leaves it open to the viewer to decide whether the injured and limp man is comatose or dead.

One image of death, *A Taube*, represents a post bombardment scene that could have been used as a propaganda image. The largely drab-coloured painting portrays a dead child outside a building, presumably his home. The young victim of war is awkwardly prostrate across the bloodstained paving stones. The word *taube*, meaning 'dove' in German, was also the British nickname for a German monoplane whose swept-back wings resembled those of a dove-like bird. In choosing this title, Nevinson alludes to the dove as a well-established symbol of innocence; the word 'dove' in English also implies a gentle, loving person, often a child. Moreover, he compares the shocking accidental death of a young innocent to that of a dove found on the pavement, while referring to the pernicious aerial bombardment delivered by this German aircraft. In reality, however, *taube* monoplanes were generally used for reconnaissance rather than bombing missions. [27]

Nevinson's 1916 Leicester Galleries exhibition of both the war's atrocities and daily routines became a paradigm of the advanced view of modern war: the war's stresses and strains from the Western Front to the home front. Recognised as innovative by both the press and the public, the one-man show sold out and became, according to more than one writer, 'the talk of London.' [28] It was extended for an additional week due to its popularity, and Nevinson would later credit much of his early success to the favourable press coverage by the notable art critics of the day, many of them friends, acquaintances or colleagues of his father. [29]

Nevinson was asked by one art critic in

cartoons, or paintings and lithographs executed in traditional styles common to Royal Academy exhibitions. If the gruesome side of war was implied, for instance, in the war cartoons, a pronounced bias for German atrocities was the only suggestion of horrible acts at the front. [23] In his 1916 exhibition, Nevinson defied those traits of similarity. Of the nearly seventy-five exhibitions of war art in Britain between 1914 and 1918, this show signified the different trend in artistic presentation of war. Frank Rutter, the forward-looking curator of the Leeds City Art Museum and an influential critic on the *Sunday Times*, noted Nevinson's importance, identifying him as 'the first British painter to give really profound and pictorial expression to the emotions aroused by the war. . . . His paintings may be a little before their time, but they are intelligible to all but the wilfully blind.' [24] At

October 1916 whether he would be repeating his success by painting more war pictures. 'No,' he replied, 'I have painted everything I saw in France, and there will be no more.' [30]

C R W Nevinson, *Twilight*, c. 1916, etching and drypoint, 7⅜ x 5⅞ inches. Department of Art, 5900.

C R W Nevinson, *A Taube*, 1916, oil on canvas, 25 x 30 inches, Department of Art, 200.

'Efforts and Ideals' and Official War Artist career

The official war artists' scheme began as a means to illustrate propaganda material distributed in Great Britain and abroad. First headed by Charles F G Masterman (1873-1927), the eminent Liberal MP and journalist, the Department of Information hired Muirhead Bone to provide drawings and prints of the war effort and Francis Dodd to paint portraits of generals and admirals. [31] Nevinson's first government-sponsored commission occurred within a scheme titled 'Efforts and Ideals'. Generating further interest abroad in the British war effort, the scheme may have been timed to confront possible civilian defeatism following the devastating losses at the Battle of the Somme in July-August 1916. [32] Whether the British propaganda efforts were so skilfully co-ordinated to the war's events is open to question; however, the 'Efforts and Ideals' series was devised to win the support of Americans, to whom the collection was distributed for sale.

One of eighteen artists employed to produce colour and black-and-white lithographs, Nevinson was commissioned in 1917 to create six 'Efforts', representations in a sub-series entitled *Building Aircraft*. Two of the images for the scheme, *In the Air* and *Banking at 4,000 Feet* conjure up the aerial view from the sides of a banking aeroplane. Balloonist artists aside, Nevinson was among the first artists to visualise the super-terrestrial drama that flight afforded. To a former proponent of Futurist ideology, the aeroplane, along with the automobile, represented the new dynamism of the advanced mechanical age discussed in the manifestos, and Nevinson must have relished the opportunity to go airborne to draw.

Both *In the Air* and *Banking at 4,000 Feet* communicate the dynamic sensation of flying in an open biplane, and Nevinson considered them to be among his best works. Invading one corner of each composition is the plane's tilted wing, shown against the seemingly limitless expanse of chequerboard fields below. The abrupt angularity in his compositions - derived from the plane's banking and swerving - conveys the queasiness and exhilaration that must have accompanied such outings in two-seater aeroplanes.

The public had seen air photographs conveying the intriguing details of fields and roads, but the vast majority of British citizens had never experienced the sensation of flying that Nevinson's views afforded. Newspapers and magazines enthusiastically reproduced his aerial views in 1917-18, and his dynamic and pioneering 'airscapes', as they were later named by

C R W Nevinson, *In the Air*, 1917, lithograph, 16 x 12 inches, Department of Art, 695.

C R W Nevinson, *Banking at 4,000 Feet*, 1917, lithograph, 15¾ x 12½ inches, Department of Art, 694.

Rutter, undoubtedly increased his popularity with the public at large. [33]

In the spring of 1917 word circulated in the press about Nevinson's pending official war artist appointment, one writer observing that: 'Three years ago, the selection of a futurist for an official job would . . . have created a riot.' [34] Nevinson, however, was clearly interested in pursuing an official position as is indicated by his correspondence with government officials in the spring of 1917 and his gift of a painting, *Swooping Down on a Hostile Plane*, to what was at that stage the National War Museum. [35] The letters written by his father to a number of influential government figures, including Masterman and Sir Alfred Mond, a Member of Parliament who also served as Chairman of the National War Museum, appear to have been critically important in his secondment as the first young, modern, official war artist. [36]

In late June 1917, Nevinson was finalising details of his contract with Masterman and his staff. Unlike Bone, he did not receive a salary but could keep his works of art and sell them after the war if he wished,

though the National War Museum had first refusal. [37] One parting statement illuminates Nevinson's perception of his role as an official artist: 'I hope I shall be able to make a fine record and that my pictures will give the civilian public some insight as to the marvellous endurance of our soldiers and the real meaning of hardships they are called upon to face' [38] Nevinson departed for France with the intention of staying three weeks, but actually stayed a month, from 5 July to 4 August 1917. He made rough sketches and drawings, some from specially-arranged aeroplane flights, before returning to a large studio on Robert Street off the Hampstead Road. He produced more than seventy-five official paintings and prints during the next seven months, one of the most prolific periods in his career. [39]

Among the earliest of his official paintings is *After a Push*, a view of a pock-marked and flooded landscape. The painting, like some of his other commissioned works, drew lukewarm responses from the government officials. After a visit to Nevinson's studio in October 1917, Thomas Derrick, the artist and Royal

C R W Nevinson, *After a Push*,
1917, oil on canvas, 22½ x 31½
inches, Department of Art, 519.

College of Art instructor who served under Masterman, reported his impressions of the first paintings: 'On the whole he appears to have avoided the more revolting aspects of the business, perhaps with the intention of gaining official approval.' Although Derrick expressed qualified praise for *After a Push*, he thought Nevinson was holding back, 'sometimes to the point of dullness'. [40] Masterman, too, was quick to react to Nevinson's first images from the commission, wondering if the artist had 'abandoned his own *metier* in order to produce *official* (perhaps dull) pictures'. Masterman reaffirmed his belief in Nevinson's talent, stating that he should 'develop his own genius — however bitter and uncompromising.' [41] Masterman and his colleagues do not appear to have anticipated the controversy that would evolve during the winter of 1917-18 when Nevinson painted in a more personal and uncompromising fashion.

Two controversial paintings in the 1918 Leicester Galleries exhibition

Nevinson worked intensely through the winter of 1917-18 in anticipation of his official war art exhibition at the Leicester Galleries in March 1918. This show coincided with the publication of *British Artists at the Front: C R W Nevinson*, a Ministry of Information volume containing seventeen reproductions of his work. Nevinson attempted to produce images that would have practical usefulness for such government publications; however, two paintings proved to be difficult for the government censor. [42]

The controversy over the first painting, *A Group of Soldiers*, began in November 1917, when Nevinson was brought to task for his portrayal of four uniformed British Tommies standing at rest. Nevinson's image suggests the reality of undernourished, exhausted, and filthy men returning from the front. Major A N Lee, the government censor responsible for vetting the official images, thought the work depicted 'the type of man . . . not worthy of the British army.' [43] He was probably more accustomed to living in the company of officers and gentlemen at a safe distance from the line. Their different vantage points led the sometimes hot-headed Nevinson to pen the following letter:

Dear Major Lee, I am writing to you to ask if you would be good enough to let me have an idea of your ideal type of manly beauty as I have just heard that you have censored one of my best pictures as 'too ugly'. When I took on this job I of course understood that my work would be submitted to a military censor but I had no idea that it would also be submitted to an aesthetic censorship. So if you would just let me know what you consider a pretty man, I will in future paint all my soldiers up to your ideal, only I must know what it is . . . . On the other hand I will not paint 'Castrated Lancelots' though I know this is how

C R W Nevinson, *A Group of Soldiers*, 1917, oil on canvas, 36 x 24 inches,
Department of Art, 520.

C R W Nevinson, *Paths of Glory*, 1917, oil on canvas, 18 x 24 inches, Department of Art, 518.

Tommies are usually represented in illustrated papers etc. – high-souled eunuchs looking mild-eyed, unable to melt butter on their tongues and mentally and physically incapable of killing a German. I refuse to insult the British army with such sentimental bilge. I might mention that all these four men in this particular picture, are portraits, men I chose quite haphazard from the Tubes as they came from France on leave …[44]

Though never sent to Lee, the letter was given to Masterman by Nevinson. The outraged artist also inquired about some form of appeals system, claiming that even the Royal Academy maintained such a body to resolve disputes surrounding matters of aesthetics. Nevinson postulated that Lee would have censored 'all Rodin, Forain, Michael Angelo, Rubens and Goya as "too ugly."[45]

Masterman appeared to side with Nevinson and intervened, stating that Lee 'should only censor things from a military point of view' rather than an artistic one.[46] The War Office would allow Nevinson to exhibit or distribute the painting privately, but it was not to be used in government publications. In conjunction with their announcement, Major Lee reiterated his concern, believing that circulation of the painting would enable the Germans, should they secure it, to use it against the British.[47]

While indecision reigned over the matter of *A Group of Soldiers*, the issue of the second offensive picture emerged. This time, however, the subject involved more than a suitable portrayal of the British troops. The censorship of *Paths of Glory* would not be resolved until the Leicester Galleries show the following March.

The brown and green painting depicts two dead British soldiers, sprawled on a littered and war-torn hillside. They appear forgotten, seemingly abandoned for some time, as their bloated bodies have begun to swell within their uniforms. An eerie, unnatural aqua light is seen in the sky, which appears only slightly at the very top of the composition. The high horizon is punctured by the skeletal web of posts and barbed wire. The mysterious light casts greenish shadows across the dead soldiers, their helmets and rifles, and the debris that surrounds them.

The first indication of a problem with the painting arose on 24 November when Masterman requested to see a painting he referred to as 'Dead Men.'[48] Five days later, Lee stated the problem with *Paths of Glory*, claiming that it would not yield 'military information to the enemy, but rather that 'the subject matter raises a point of policy'.[49]

Consultation within the War Office and later meetings between the government officials and the two Nevinsons occurred in December 1917. Although no record of their discussion survives, the Nevinsons were most likely told that 'representations of the dead have an ill effect at home.'[50] This may have been in reference to the images of the dead that appeared in the film *The Battle of the Somme* of August 1916, an association that Nevinson had raised with Masterman on 3 December.[51]

The censorship battle continued unresolved, and uncertainty surrounding his future employment remained ever doubtful. The months of December 1917 and January 1918 were anxious ones for Nevinson who feared a return to battle should he fail in the official war artists' programme while the government was calling up some of the discharged soldiers and previously rejected men to replenish the drastically depleted ranks at the front.[52]

The censorship issue came to a head during Nevinson's second Leicester Galleries show, opened by the newly-appointed Minister of Information, Lord Beaverbrook, on 1 March. Nevinson displayed *Paths of Glory* along with the other fifty-eight works of art. However, he disguised the dead bodies with a diagonally positioned piece of brown paper, upon which he had written 'CENSORED.' The press photographed the partially-hidden painting and writers pondered what lay under the banner. Its significance and the undue attention that it produced in both the gallery and the press resulted in the painting's eventual removal. It is not clear whether this was done by the government, the Leicester Galleries, or the artist himself.[53]

The specific reasons for the censorship of *Paths of Glory* have never been clearly established. The representation of war-related deaths, as in *A Taube*, had not been a problem for the government censor earlier;

Photograph of *Paths of Glory* with "CENSORED" banner, printed in the *Daily Mail*, 2 March 1918.

C R W Nevinson (right) with Lord Beaverbrook, at the Agnew Galleries, London, May 1918. IWM FLM 2469.

panoramic colour war photographs containing dead soldiers were on display at the Grafton Galleries, while Nevinson's controversial image was hanging nearby.[54] The most probable reason for the censorship concerns the title of the painting and its associations with the well-known Thomas Gray poem, 'Elegy Written in a Country Churchyard.' Drawn from the fourth line of the ninth stanza - 'The paths of glory lead but to the grave' - the title suggests a cynical interpretation of the meditative classic of English literature. Given the hardships and sacrifices suffered by many British families during the more than three years of war - the casualty rate approaching its end-of-war total of 745,000 British dead and almost two million others wounded - the government's hesitation in sanctioning and distributing such a powerful image is not surprising.[55] The Battle of Passchendaele had only finished in November, and the potential for social unrest at home was not insignificant.

C R W Nevinson,
The Harvest of Battle, 1919,
oil on canvas, 72 x 125 inches,
Department of Art, 1921.

An increasingly disillusioned home front now having to queue for food rations, a growing militancy amongst labour organisations after the strikes of 1917, and the political and economic uncertainties following the Russian Revolution may have entered the minds of the government officials who appraised this harsh view of war during the bleak winter of 1917-18. [56]

Hall of Remembrance painting

Despite his problems within the Ministry of Information, Nevinson was commissioned to paint a large picture for the British government in the spring of 1918. His painting, along with approximately forty works by other artists, was overseen by the British War Memorials Committee and intended for permanent exhibition in the Hall of Remembrance. The commemorative building paying tribute to the war dead was never realised, in part owing to the disbandment of the Ministry at the end of the war. [57]

Robert Ross, an adviser to the British War Memorials Committee, first suggested the commissioning of several paintings of uniform size, each recording a different aspect of the war effort, both at home and abroad. His proposed size, 72 x 125 inches, was that of each of Paolo Uccello's three fifteenth century scenes of *The Battle of San Romano*, one of which hung in the National Gallery. [58]

In his letter to Ross, Nevinson expressed interest in the subject of a field casualty station, 'as I feel most competent to do this side of war as I became familiar with it in the Ranks and it is the side that interests and moves me the most.' Nevinson sought permission to return to France in order to tour casualty stations, and the government granted him a long-weekend visit in December 1918. [59]

Conceived in the nineteenth-century tradition of war-painting, his 'Uccello-sized' *The Harvest of Battle* employs a long horizontal format for describing the endless line of men in transit and the evacuation of the wounded. The high horizon line is broken by the smoke from explosions and shellfire. In its panoramic presentation of soldiers and war-torn land, Nevinson's painting resembles the battle pictures of Douglas Giles (1857-1923) and others who portrayed colonial conflicts in the Sudan and elsewhere in the 1880s. [60]

The Harvest of Battle employs compositional elements of earlier Nevinson paintings: pools of stagnant water as in *After a Push*; barbed wire and debris including dead bodies, as in *Paths of Glory*; and the transporting of the wounded as in *Twilight*. In June 1919, Nevinson was asked to write about his painting before its government distribution and he provided the following description:

A typical scene after an offensive at dawn. Walking wounded, prisoners, and stretcher cases are making their way to the rear through the water-logged country of Flanders. By now, the infantry have advanced behind the creeping barrage on the right, only leaving the dead, mud, and wire; but their former positions are now occupied by the Artillery. The enemy is sending up SOS signals and once more these shattered men will be subjected to counter-battery fire. [61]

Unlike many nineteenth-century battle artists, Nevinson

produced an anti-heroic rather than heroic view of war. An emaciated soldier's body lies with its bent head confronting the viewer in the foreground; two additional bodies slump on the edges of nearby pools of water. In the middle ground, scores of soldiers move equipment and infirm comrades across a semi-flooded battlefield. Some soldiers bear the injured on stooped shoulders, others with the aid of a stretcher, across a denuded landscape; seemingly helpless in their search for medical attention, they proceed across a disfigured terrain while barrage fire continues in the distance. As Nevinson's final government commission of the war, the 1919 commemorative tribute was designed to hang with the other 'Uccello-sized' paintings, *The Menin Road* by Paul Nash, *A Battery Shelled* by Wyndham Lewis, and *A Shell Dump, France* by William Roberts among others, along with the centrepiece of the Hall of Remembrance, *Gassed* by John Singer Sargent. [62]

Though less innovative than his pre-commission war art and lacking the dynamic futurist-fracturing that in part contributed to his popularity, Nevinson's *The Harvest of Battle* and many other official views of the First World War succeeded in their aim; as artistic records of the endurance of British soldiers along the Western Front. Considering Nevinson's traumatic beginning in 1914-15 as one of the first artists to witness the carnage and futility of trench warfare, his personal commitment to the war was the longest of any official war artist. His re-direction of artistic priorities and interests is hardly surprising given all that he had seen during these eventful years. The change in style may also have been an emotional necessity, as he may have wished to distance himself from his pre-1914 Futurist ideals. This change is also in keeping with the wartime avant-garde painters in Paris who moved away from abstract configurations in their work and returned to more legible and orderly compositions.

During the immediate post-war years, Nevinson created representational modernist paintings and prints of Parisian interiors and English landscapes. Following his first visit to the United States in 1919, he produced prints of New York streets, skyscrapers, and bridges for his November-December 1920 exhibition at the Bourgeois Galleries. This New York one-man show, entitled 'The Old World and the New,' attracted large crowds but mixed reviews, probably in part due to the aggressive statements in his public lectures and his condescending views quoted in the press interviews. In Britain, Nevinson's name became a household word, dominating the London art and social pages throughout the nineteen twenties and nineteen thirties. In explaining

his popularity to an Australian audience in 1931, Konody wrote:

> He had become famous overnight and was discussed by people who had never seen any of his work. Interviews and reporters kept the ball rolling. To-day, in any controversial question on art, Nevinson's opinion is listened to in preference to that of the President of the Royal Academy whose very name, by the way, is not known to the vast majority of educated Englishmen. [63]

Despite the perseverance and artistic acumen that produced an extraordinarily prolific record of war, Nevinson was unable to sustain the vitality and resonance of success this early. Rutter wrote that Nevinson 'is at his best when he is painting something he greatly hates'. [64] Unlike his official- artist colleagues, Paul Nash and Stanley Spencer, who would expand their artistic investigations and continue to pursue innovative and experimental means of self-expression, Nevinson produced cautious and largely uninspired work after 1925. With the exception of his limited service as a stretcher-bearer in North London during the Blitz, Nevinson was never again confronted by such horror as the First World War, and much of his post-war art reflects this safe distance from its trauma, anguish, and inspiration.

Notes

All primary sources from the Department of Art, Nevinson Files, are abbreviated ART-NEV.

1. Department of Art, Papers of the British Permanent Memorials Committee, Bennett Memo, 9 March 1918.
2. See L G Wickham Legg and E T Williams, eds, *Dictionary of National Biography, 1941-1950*, Oxford University Press, Oxford, 1971, pp 619 - 21; Olive Banks, *The Biographical Dictionary of British Feminists, Volume One: 1800-1930*, Wheatsheaf, Brighton, 1985, pp 136 - 39.
3. C R W Nevinson, *Paint and Prejudice*, Methuen, London, pp 46 - 52.
4. Marinetti's 'The Founding and Manifesto of Futurism' originally appeared in *Le Figaro* (Paris), 20 February 1909. See it reprinted in Umbro Apollonio, *Futurist Manifestos*, Thames and Hudson, London, 1970, pp 19 - 24.
5. 'Vital English Art', *Observer*, 7 June 1914; also reprinted in C R W Nevinson, op cit, pp 58 - 60.
6. H W Nevinson Journals, Bodleian Library, Oxford University: e.618/3, 25 October 1914, p 65.
7. *Returning to the Trenches* (1914?-15), oil on canvas, 20 x 30 inches, National Gallery of Canada, 4800.
8. P G Konody, *Observer*, 14 March 1915.
9. See H W Nevinson Journals: e.618/3, 7 November 1914, p 76; 10 November 1914, p 77; 12 November 1914, p 79; 13 November 1914, p 79; 14 November 1914, p 80. Nevinson

Senior stayed in Flanders until 23 December 1914.

10. The incident occurred at Woesten, approximately 10 km NW of Ypres. H W Nevinson Journals: e.618/3, 24 November 1914, p 85.

11. Meaburn Tatham and James E Miles, eds., *Friends' Ambulance Unit. 1914-1919. A Record*, Swarthmore, London, [1920], p 7.

12. C R W Nevinson, op cit, p 74.

13. See C W H Havard, *Black's Medical Dictionary*, 35th ed., A & C Black, London, 1987, pp 585 - 89.

14. See C H H Burleigh's *Interior of the Pavilion. Brighton* (c 1915), oil on canvas, 22 x 18 inches, Art Department, 116.

15. *La Patrie* (1916), oil on canvas, 23 x 35 1/2 inches, Birmingham City Museum and Art Gallery, 1988-P-104.

16. H W Nevinson Journals: e. 619/1, 1 June 1915, p 12.

17. C R W Nevinson, op cit, pp 78 - 79; *Gazette*, October 1917, p 21.

18. C R W Nevinson, op cit, p 78.

19. Ibid, p 79; *In the Observation Ward*, oil on canvas, 16 x 12 inches, is illustrated in P G Konody, *Modern War: Paintings of C R W Nevinson*, Grant Richards, London, 1917, p 49.

20. C R W Nevinson, op cit, p 82. *La Mitrailleuse* (1915), oil on canvas, 24 x 20 inches, Tate Gallery, 3177.

21. *Christian Science Monitor*, 13 October 1916.

22. *Daily Mirror*, 29 May 1916.

23. Note previous Leicester Galleries catalogues: *Exhibition of War Satires by Will Dyson, with an Introductory Note by H G Wells* (January 1915); "*Germany at Work.*" *Catalogue of an Exhibition of Paintings, Drawings and Lithographs by Joseph Pennell with notes by the artist* (March 1916); and *The "Punch" War Cartoons by Bernard Partridge, L Raven-Hill and F H Townsend*, (April 1916).

24. *Sunday Times*, 24 September 1916. Another reviewer described Nevinson's paintings as 'ruthlessly truth-telling . . . [which] rank among the more illuminating documents of the war.' *Nation*, 30 September 1916.

25. *Sunday Times*, 31 December 1916.

26. See Leicester Galleries, *Catalogue of an Exhibition of Paintings and Drawings of War by C R W Nevinson. Introduction by General Sir Ian Hamilton*, London, September - October 1916.

27. Nevinson later claimed: 'Dunkirk was one of the first towns to suffer aerial bombardment, and I was one of the first men to see a child who had been killed by it. There the small body lay before me, a symbol of all that was to come.' C R W Nevinson, op cit, p 76.

28. Charles Lewis Hind, 'An Appreciation,' in Bourgeois Galleries, *The Old World and the New. Exhibition of Paintings. Lithographs and Woodcuts by C R W Nevinson of London. England* (New York: 8 November - 4 December 1920); C R W Nevinson, op cit, p 85.

29. Among these helpful critics were Frank Rutter, Lewis Hind, and P G Konody. C R W Nevinson, op cit, p 85.

30. *Daily Mirror*, 18 October 1916.

31. For further discussion of the official war artists' programme, see Meirion and Susie Harries, *The War Artists: British Official War Art in the Twentieth Century*, Michael Joseph in association with the Imperial War Museum and Tate Gallery, London, 1983.

32. Ibid, p 78.

33. Aerial photographs were reproduced in *Flight* magazine (11 December 1914, for example) and other periodicals; Rutter, *Arts Gazette*, 28 June 1919.

34. *Sunday Pictorial*, 1 July 1917.

35. ART-NEV: Nevinson to Mond, 30 April 1917, p 242; *Swooping Down on a Hostile Plane* (1917), oil on canvas, 24 x 18 inches, Art Department, 517.

36. ART-NEV: H W Nevinson to Masterman, 1 May 1917, p 243; H W Nevinson Journals: e.620/2, 1 May 1917, p 43 and 8 May 1917. Nevinson was also hired by the Canadian War Memorials Fund to produce an official painting, *War in the Air*, for their government programme. See Maria Tippett, *Art at the Service of War - Canada, Art, and the Great War*, University of Toronto Press, Toronto, 1984, for a thorough account of the programme.

37. ART-NEV: Ministry of Information to Nevinson, 30 June 1917, p 224.

38. ART-NEV: Nevinson to Masterman, 30 June 1917, pp 222 - 23.

39. C R W Nevinson, op. cit., p 106.

40. ART-NEV: Derrick to Masterman, 16 October 1917, pp 191 - 92.

41. ART-NEV: Masterman to Hudson, 29 October 1917, p 181.

42. See Leicester Galleries, *Catalogue of an Exhibition of Pictures of War by C R W Nevinson*, London, March 1918. The Department of Information became the Ministry of Information in February 1918.

43. Quoted in Harries, op cit, pp 44 - 45.

44. ART-NEV: Nevinson to Lee, undated, pp 148 - 51.

45. ART-NEV: Nevinson to Masterman, 25 November 1917, p 147.

46. ART-NEV: Masterman to Nevinson, 26 November 1917, p 145 and Masterman to Lee, 27 November 1917, p 144.

47. ART-NEV: Lee to Masterman, 13 December 1917, p 124. Lee was clearly at odds with Nevinson, as evidenced by the Lee-Yockney correspondence. Of the occasional bad press associated with the 1918 Leicester Galleries exhibition and criticism of the artist's preface in the catalogue, Lee said that Nevinson 'certainly deserves all he gets' and went on to refer to Nevinson's painting as a 'Group of Brutes'. Lee-Yockney Correspondence: 3 March 1918, 7050 .705, and 23 March 1918, 7050.706, Nevinson Collection, Archive of Modern British Art in the Tate Gallery, London.

48. ART-NEV: Yockney to Nevinson, 24 November 1917, p 152.

49. ART-NEV: Lee to Yockney, 29 November 1917, p 138.

50. H W Nevinson Journals: e.620/3, 5 December 1917, p 24 and ARTNEV: Yockney to Masterman, 4 December 1917, p 129. See other documents, ART-NEV: Lee to Yockney, 6 December 1917, p 127, and ART-NEV: Memo from Yockney to Masterman, 6 December 1917, p 126.

51. Department of Film, 191. For a full discussion of the film, see Nicholas Reeves, *Official British Film Propaganda During the First World War*, Croom Helm in association with the Imperial War Museum, London, 1986, pp 101 - 3, 157 - 64, 243 - 47.

52. 'The Military Service (Review of Exceptions) Act of 1917' received the Royal Assent on 5 April 1917. See *The Public General Acts, 1917-1918*, Eyre and Spottiswoode, London, (1918), chapter 12, pp 13 - 15; also *Times*, 25 October 1917, p 10d and *Times*, 29 October 1917, p 3c.

53. *Daily Mail*, 2 March 1918. For further discussion of the censorship issue, see Charles E Doherty, 'Nevinson's Elegy: "Paths of Glory,"' *Art Journal*, Spring 1992, vol 51, no. 1, pp 64 - 71.

54. This photography exhibition was frequently reviewed along with Nevinson's one-man show. See one review containing a photograph with dead bodies in 'British Battles in Photography. The Camera as War Correspondent,' in *Graphic*, 9 March 1918, p 293.

55. Arthur Marwick, *The Deluge: British Society and the First World War*, Bodley Head, London, 1965, p 290.

56. Ibid, pp 189, 194 - 197; John Stevenson, *British Society 1914 - 45*, Penguin Books, London, 1984, pp 72

- 75, 87 - 88; and John Turner, *British Politics and the Great War. Coalition and Conflict 1915-1918*, New Haven and London, Yale University Press, 1992, pp 52 - 53, 202.

57. See Harries, op. cit., pp 91 - 94, 114 - 17.

58. Department of Art, 460a/10, Papers of the British War Memorials Committee, Ross Letter, 8 April 1918; and 486/12, Meeting Minutes, 19 June 1918. The BWMC members included Lord Beaverbrook, Lord Rothermere, Bennett, Yockney and Mond.

59. ART-NEV: Nevinson to Ross, 21 April 1918, pp 56 - 59; ART-NEV: Yockney to Nevinson, 20 August 1918, p 27; ART-NEV: Nevinson to Yockney, 21 December 1918, pp 2 - 4.

60. See the two Giles paintings depicting the York and Lancaster Regiments in *The Battle of Tamaai. 13 March 1884, 1884*, oils on canvas, 41 3/8 x 72 inches, National Army Museum.

61. ART-NEV: Nevinson to Yockney, 11 June 1919, pp 169 - 70.

62. All paintings now reside in the Art Department.

63. P G Konody, 'The Art of C R W Nevinson,' *Art in Australia*, 15 February 1931, p 21.

64. Quoted in Pontus Hulten, *Futurism and Futurisms*, Abbeville Press, New York, 1986, p 529.

Further Reading

Richard Cork, *Vorticism and Abstract Art in the First Machine Age*, Gordon Fraser, London, 1976.

C R W Nevinson, 1889 - 1946. Retrospective Exhibition of Paintings, Drawings and Prints, Kettles Yard, Cambridge, 10 September - 9 October 1988.

Samuel Hynes, *A War Imagined: The First World War and English Culture*, Atheneum, New York, 1991.

Acknowledgements

Special thanks are due to Suzanne Bardgett, Peter Simkins, Angela Weight, and Jenny Wood for their help with this article; to the *Daily Mail* for kind permission to reproduce the photograph of *Paths of Glory* with 'Censored' banner; and to the staff members of the Archive of Modern British Art at the Tate Gallery.

Nobody's child: a brief history of the tactical use of Vickers machine-guns in the British Army, 1914-1918

Chris McCarthy

Chris McCarthy is a conservation officer in the Department of Exhibits and Firearms.

In 1934 Major E W N Wade, writing in the Army Quarterly, recalled an incident from the early months of the Great War. Orders to advance to the front line had brought his battalion to an exposed position in the middle of a gigantic beet field:

> An incident in connection with this impossible position will always remain in my memory. One morning a very distinguished officer visited me and remarked that the guns and teams appeared to be in a rather exposed place - to all of which I agreed. He then surprised me by jumping up on top of the gun emplacement, in full view of the enemy, picking up a withered beet and exclaiming, 'You must replant these around the gun positions, water them, then the enemy won't know that you are here!'. My section sergeant's face was a sight for the blind. [1]

This article looks at the development of Vickers machine-gun tactics from this early example of naivety to the sophisticated tactical weapon it became by the end of the war.

1914: early lessons

At the start of the war the British Army possessed 1,858 Maxim machine-guns in service and reserve. These were the type of gun used in the South African war, heavy and prone to stoppages and due shortly to be replaced by the Vickers gun, which was lighter and more reliable. 105 of the new guns had been delivered to the army at the outbreak of war. On 11 August 1914, the War Office placed an order with Vickers for 192 guns, increasing it to 1,792 in September. The order was to be delivered by July 1915, at a rate of fifty a month. In September the order was further increased to 200 a month or as many as could be produced, and the following February an order was placed in America [where orders had been placed before the war] for 2,000 guns. [2]

In 1914 the Army organised its machine-guns in 'sections' of two guns per infantry battalion. The section complement consisted of one officer, one sergeant and 16 other ranks. The guns were carried in a General Service limbered wagon, together with the mounts and 14 boxes, each containing 600 rounds of ammunition. [3] Originally the crew was four men to a gun.

Filling cartridge belts for machine-guns. The man on the right is packing the newly filled belts into boxes. Q61573

The number one - usually an NCO - had charge of the gun and fired it, the number two fed the belts into the gun, while the other numbers carried ammunition and reloaded the belts. This account by George Coppard, a private in the Machine-gun Corps whose memoir of the First World War was published by the Imperial War Museum in 1969, describes how the gun crews were trained for deploying the guns in action:

> The standard drill for going into action was complicated, and long and hard practice was needed to get a team into really good shape. On the blow of a whistle, Number One dashed forward with the tripod, released the ratchet-held legs [sic] so that they swung forward, both pointing outwards, and secured them rigidly by tightening the ratchet handles. Sitting down, he removed two metal pins from the head of the tripod, whereupon Number Two placed the gun in position on the tripod. Number One whipped in the pins and the gun was ready for loading. Number Three dashed forward with an ammunition box containing a canvas belt, pocketed to hold 250 rounds. Number Two inserted the brass tag-end of the belt into the feed-block on the right side of the gun. Number One grabbed the tag-end poking through the left side, jerked it through, at the same time pulling back the crank handle twice, which completed the loading operation. For sighting, the flick of a finger sprang the stem

of the rear sight into a vertical position, and a rapid selection of ranges was provided by a spring-loaded wheel, turned up or down as necessary. Part of the drill when practising on the butts was to knock over steel target plates, and we were expected to do this by accuracy of aim, and not by watching the dirt fly as a guide to the target. [4]

Numbers Three and Four were responsible for getting ammunition up to the gun, and loading the belts. The belts were loaded by hand or by means of an apparatus not dissimilar to an old fashioned meat mincer. The rounds were fed into the hopper on top of the machine. It gathered the round from the hopper and located the bullet into the canvas belt fed in underneath the hopper. The machine was operated by a hand crank. Whilst sounding - and looking - somewhat 'Heath Robinson', it appears to have worked very well. Charles Baxter, an ex-member of the Corps, interviewed by the Museum's Department of Sound Records, recalled that when first issued the ammunition had been clipped - 'Five in a clip like you used for a rifle', but later they came unclipped in boxes of a thousand. 'We had a little sausage machine,' Baxter described, 'and we kept dropping them in - that's how we filled the belts. But the biggest trouble we had with them belts was they were canvas and if they got wet, you'd get a block'. [5]

To combat this problem of damp belts, a disposable link belt was developed, made of pressed steel. It appears to have worked well, but was used mainly by the Royal Flying Corps who also used Vickers guns in their aircraft, and was seldom encountered in the trenches.

The first Victoria Crosses of the war were won by machine-gunners of the 4th Battalion, Royal Fusiliers at the Battle of Mons. A company of Fusiliers, with a machine-gun section, was defending the Nimy Bridge across the Mons canal. The defenders came under a withering fire from the advancing German Army and their position became almost desperate. The gun was sited in an exposed position and the crews were constantly being knocked out. Each time the gun stopped, Lieutenant Maurice Dease crossed the open ground to the gun to see what was wrong. This he did a number of times, and, despite being badly wounded twice, would not leave his post. A third wound proved fatal.

The gun was taken over by Private Godley, who manned it single-handed for over two hours, in which time he too received two serious wounds. After

Gun team of the 33rd Battalion Machine-Gun Corps in Passchendaele Church position. Machine-gun belts can been seen hanging up to dry. Q56259

covering the retreat of the rest of the company, he disabled the guns and threw the parts into the canal. Taken prisoner by the Germans, he learnt in a POW camp that he had been awarded the VC. [6]

By December 1914 the need for more trained machine-gunners was starting to become urgent. It was decided to open a Machine-gun School at Caserne d'Abret in St Omer. The commandant was Major C D'A B S Baker-Carr, a retired Rifle Brigade officer, who had once served as an Assistant Instructor at the School of Musketry in Hythe. He had two Quartermaster-Sergeant instructors as his staff, whose first students were themselves to train as instructors. The Artists Rifles [28th Bn County of London Regiment] was asked to supply sixteen suitable men. It duly did and on 1 December 1914 the chosen candidates reported for a crash course of fourteen days. [7] In this short time they had to learn how the gun worked, how to deal with stoppages and the deployment of the Maxim and Vickers machine-guns. Sixteen men was the optimum number, that is to say eight men round each of the two Maxim guns which they had managed to borrow from the 2nd Battalion Royal Irish Rifles.

On 14 December the first course got under way, consisting of 8 Officers and 120 other ranks. In April 1915 the school was moved to the Benedictine Convent at Wisques, some four miles north-west of St Omer. By the end of May, 280 officers and men were passing through it each month. [8]

1915: building

In February 1915, the number of machine-guns per infantry battalion was raised from two to four.

In the early years, the machine-gun was used for purely direct fire. That is to say it only engaged targets at which it could be directly pointed. This meant that the

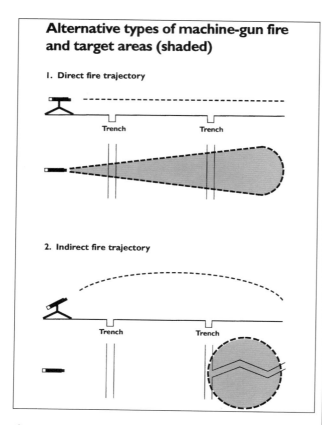

Alternative types of machine-gun fire and target areas (shaded)

1. Direct fire trajectory

Trench   Trench

2. Indirect fire trajectory

Trench   Trench

Alternative types of machine-gun fire and target areas (shaded)

guns were used individually by the most forward troops, usually in the very front line. A typical use for machine-guns at this time was in sweeping the German parapet at night to harass sentries and patrols, and in interrupting wiring parties engaged in repairing the wire in which the artillery had blown holes during the day. [9]

The aim was to cover every yard of ground the enemy might attack over by the firing of at least one machine-gun firing on a flank, its own front being covered by other machine-guns. There was a move afoot to group machine-guns in strong-points usually called 'Keeps'. These were groups of trenches adapted to all-round defence and located in the reserve line, but in practice such Keeps rarely had enough guns.

Both the Vickers and the lighter and more portable Lewis guns were used indiscriminately at this time. Increased supplies of the Vickers guns released the Lewis gun to the infantry as direct support weapons.

In August 1915, owing partly to a very considerable increase in the supplies of Vickers guns and partly to a realisation of the tactical differences between the Lewis Gun and the Vickers, Brigade machine-gun companies came into being, with their own commanders and HQ. This change solved some problems, notably in supply and control, but created others, particularly in the sphere of promotion, seniority, reinforcements and 'attached men'. [10] These problems were not solved until the formation of the actual Machine-Gun Corps with its own structure which enabled the specialist machine-gunner to be judged by his peers and not by infantry standards. The new organisation appealed to reason but not to sentiment, divorcing the machine-gunners still more from their own battalions and comrades.

The portability of the Lewis gun was soon appreciated and it was in this role - in support of attacking infantry - that the battalion machine-gun section, armed with Lewis guns, came into being, still under the control of the battalion commander.

It soon became clear that the infantry would be unable to keep up the supply of personnel to man the guns, and in October 1915 the Machine-Gun Corps was formed. Each tactical unit took the number of the brigade to which it was attached. Thus the company attached to 140th Brigade became the 140th Machine-Gun Company. Each company comprised a headquarters and four sections, each of four guns. In turn, each gun had a crew of four men, though this proved to be inadequate in times of great activity, such as when the guns were used in support of an attack. [11]

At the battle of Loos in September 1915 the 9th [Scottish] Division initiated a tactical first. Each of the infantry battalions had four machine-guns that advanced with the attacking troops, while fourteen were 'brigaded' in the rear of the front line to co-operate with the artillery. [12]

It had been slowly realised that with the build-up of artillery and ammunition the destructive power of a barrage would increase, and that in the event of a bombardment of the front line trench, little of the trench would remain. To counter this, the principle of 'defence in depth' was applied, the front line trench itself being lightly held and the machine-guns placed in the reserve trenches. This departure was unpopular with the infantry, who were still expected to hold the front line trench at any cost, and would have preferred to have their machine-guns closer to hand.

1916: refining

Early in 1916 'harassing fire' at night was adopted. It soon became a regular feature of trench life, but at this time there was no thought of using it in the event of an enemy attack. Harassing fire was indirect fire from the reserve positions together with that of many of the guns in the front line directed at known supply dumps, tracks, communication trenches and headquarters. The number of rounds fired by a company might be anything from a thousand rounds on a quiet night to ten or twenty thousand on the eve of a raid or an offensive. [13]

In March 1916 it was announced that an additional machine-gun company was to be added to each division, as soon as weapons and personnel became available, creating a 'divisional machine-gun company' under the command of the division, whilst the remaining companies would stay under the command of the brigade commanders.

The summer brought the Battle of the Somme, and the first real blooding of the new Corps. Orders issued for the first day concerning the machine-guns were as follows:

10. Infantry, machine-guns and trench mortars will co-operate in this task [harassing personnel] and in keeping open the wire cut...

14. Special arrangements will be made in each division to cover every stage of further advance of the infantry by machine-gun fire, indirect where necessary. Rifle fire from the enemy's trenches during the advance will be kept down by fire from Vickers and Lewis guns, firing enfilade as far as possible, otherwise by using overhead fire.[14]

It will be clear from the above that commanders were still not using the machine gun to its full potential.

The taking of Beaumont Hamel by the 51st [Highland] Division, shows how much the British Army had learnt over the five months of the battle. The division placed the bulk of its guns just east of Auchonvillers, near a tumulus called the Bowery. From here they fired a continuous barrage on the German third line and continued it back to the heights behind the village. This was designed to stop the enemy from using their machine-guns against the attacking Scotsmen and also to hamper him in bringing up reserves and supplies.

This was the first occasion on which the Division had employed machine-guns to fire an overhead barrage during the attack. The men were accordingly specially warned that the enormous volume of bullets passing over their heads would suggest that they were only a few inches above the crowns of their steel helmets,

Machine-guns in action at Mouquet Farm on the Somme, September 1916. The team on the right are using a captured German gun. This practice was quite common when the guns were available. Q1419

Canadian machine-gunners in a shell hole, Vimy Ridge, April 1917. CO1146

Men of the 1st Leicester Regiment [6th Division] with a section of machine-guns in a captured 2nd line trench. Ribecourt, 20 November 1917. Q6279

A Machine-Gun Corps parade at Rombly, on 13 May 1918. Note the ammunition belts stretched out in front of the gun. Q3272

whereas in reality there would be a margin of safety of many feet. This warning proved to be a sound precaution: the bullets did seem unpleasantly close and might well have created despondency and alarm. [15]

At the end of the year many of the Divisions had received their fourth machine-gun company, later to be known as the Divisional Company. Coinciding with this, the need was realised for a Divisional Machine-Gun Commander, to control and co-ordinate the brigade machine-guns, much as the artillery was controlled. This met with considerable opposition from the infantry commanders who did not want to lose control of their guns. In fact, a machine-gun officer rather than a commander was appointed who became responsible for all the machine-guns in the Division. He was to command the Divisional company and act only as an adviser to the other companies. At the same time a Corps machine-gun officer was appointed to advise each Corps. This

development left the real control of the guns with the divisional staff, thus enabling the guns to be used as a group more easily.

1917: exploiting

Guns in the trenches were now grouped into subsections of two guns. This had the advantage of simplifying relief and gave better control to the officers and NCOs in charge of the guns. Two guns were also better able to support each other if attacked, and particularly if out-flanked.

By the Battle of Arras in April 1917 the machine-gun barrage was a standard element in the offensive build-up. The Canadians had for some time committed much thought and care to their machine-gun organisation and tactics and this came to fruition with their highly successful attack on Vimy Ridge. 'The overhead machine-gun barrages had been valuable', wrote the official historian [of the war in France and Flanders] 'in giving confidence to the attack and, at least at some points, cowing the enemy defence. This was not the first battle in which the heavy machine-gun had been employed in this manner, but it may be said to have been that which established its use as an offensive weapon'. [16]

Barrage fire was really the birth of offensive machine-gun tactics. It took the Vickers gun out of the direct support role under the control of the infantry and made it a Divisional weapon for attacks. At this time it also became apparent that guns should be deployed in depth in both defence and attack. Utilising both direct and indirect fire, this was achieved by allotting the available guns into forward and rear guns. The forward guns were given the tasks of giving immediate support to the attacking infantry and the consolidation of captured ground, whilst the rear guns supplied long range covering fire. It must be remembered that this was still the time of trench warfare and limited objectives, so it was generally possible to site the rear guns where they could cover the advance without moving their position more than once.

In defence, the forward guns were to defend the outpost positions by direct fire, while the rear guns defended specific areas with direct fire and if possible, as a secondary task, supported the troops in the more forward positions. There were no fixed rules about how many guns were in each group, but the advanced guns were kept to a minimum, to retain the defence in depth theory.

By the Battle of Messines in June 1917 the machine-gun barrage was built into the artillery preparation. As can be seen below, the benefit of massed weapons had not been lost on the High Command and, employed with a vengeance through meticulous planning and careful use of intelligence, turned out to be a complete success.

The machine-gun barrage was to be laid in conjunction with the artillery barrage, lifting 400 yards ahead of the artillery's creeping shrapnel barrage. This would involve 454 machine-guns, out of a total of over 700. The ammunition allotted for the first two days of the attack was a staggering fifteen million rounds; three million for harassing fire, six million for barrages and six million for SOS calls.

The same tactics were employed for the rest of 1917, with reasonable success. The main problem was with the administration of the newly-formed Corps. The Divisional Machine-gun Officer was expected to be responsible for the discipline and training of the machine-gun companies and yet he had no executive power over them, even to the point of being unable to give an order to a brigade company without first obtaining the permission of the brigadier concerned. The situation was not helped by the abolition of the post of Corps machine-gun officer in July 1917.

Having a machine-gun company attached to each infantry brigade was found to be wasteful. In January 1918, General Headquarters relented and divisional machine-gun battalions were formed, enabling the power of the massed machine-guns to be deployed on the divisional front, where they were more effective. This meant on the entire divisional front rather than in strict support of each brigade where they might be under-used. The brigade and battalion commanders initially did not like the arrangement, but soon came round to the idea. To reinforce this change, the Divisional Machine-Gun Officer, who was an adviser, was replaced by a Commander who was also an adviser. An inspector of machine-gun units was appointed at GHQ with the rank of Brigadier General. He was supported at each Army headquarters by a deputy inspector with the rank of Colonel.

1918: winning

The Corps was beginning to take shape as a separate fighting force, the command structure being reinforced in February by the reinstatement of the Corps Machine-Gun Officer, brought back as the machine-gunners felt they did not have sufficient 'clout' at HQ. There appears to have been a tussle over the post at GHQ level throughout the rest of the war. [17]

At this time there was much debate over the manpower shortage: how many men were actually available for the BEF and how could they best be used? Should they be sent to the traditional infantry and artillery or channelled to the new technology, notably tanks and aircraft, but also machine-guns and trench mortars?

While the debate continued, the Germans launched their Michael offensive on 21 March 1918.

With the entire BEF fighting for its life, there are numerous accounts of units fighting to the last man, and the machine-gun battalions were no exception. Here is a typical account of an action giving some idea of the confused nature of the fighting. It tells the story of the machine-guns in the retreat of the 34th Division. The action took place around Croisilles on 21 March 1918:

The Machine-gun Battalion had two guns of "A" and eight of "C" Company in this portion of the first system. The sole survivors of teams

Machine-gunners of the 23rd Battalion Machine-Gun Corps, sighting barrage battery position. They are using a prismatic compass and Barr & Stroud range finding instrument.

Men of the Machine-Gun Corps firing a Vickers machine-gun in an anti-aircraft role. Q5172

C/40, 41, in Valley Support, were Second Lieutenant Percy and a Private, who carried his severely wounded officer to the aid post. Nothing was ever heard of Second Lieutenant Lloyd and the teams of C/44, 45 were last seen under Second Lieutenant Stanson, constructing a bombing block in Queen's Lane, the enemy being in Tiger Trench behind them. Sergeant Browning, in command of guns C/46 47, fired till the enemy were within bombing distance. One team was overpowered; the other, reduced to three men, got their gun away to Factory, but lost it there in a hand to hand scrap. Guns A/48, 49, in Hump support, were buried by a shell in the morning, but were dug out and were in action by two p.m. A little later the enemy suddenly appeared on the parados, and number two of 48 was shot. The guns were got away to Factory Avenue, whence they did execution on masses of the enemy in the valley south of Croisilles. Later they went with the Royal Scots to the second system and did splendid work. On 22nd, gun 49 was blown to pieces by shell, and Second-Lieutenant Paton and gun 48, with its team, was last seen fighting somewhere in the second system.[18]

After the German Spring and Summer offensives had been successfully contained, and the Battle of Amiens had begun, there was a general return to open warfare. The tactical control over machine-guns returned to the brigades and battalions in the field. By and large the machine-gun officers were left free to assist the advance in whatever ways they could, either by overhead covering fire or by pushing forward in close support, or even in advance of the infantry and employing direct fire. Below is an example from the New Zealand Machine-gun Battalion in the later months of 1918 illustrating the opportunistic style of open warfare:

> In the great advance of 1918 the Wellington Company were involved in what could only be described as a turkey shoot. From a Brigade observation post the whole countryside was full of enemy troops. The machine-gunners pushed forward in advance of the brigade to take full advantage of the situation, set their guns up and started the carnage. At first they concentrated on transport , lorries and limbered wagons. Later they directed their fire to field guns. They had not had such an opportunity before and they made the most of it. One gunner aptly remarked "Its like shooting tame ducks". [19]

With the advent of open warfare the crews no longer had to manhandle the guns, equipment and ammunition across shell-torn terrain and trenches, but were able to put to use their limbers, to carry the guns and equipment. This enabled crews and guns to keep pace with the infantry and provide invaluable fire power to support the advancing troops.

The battalion organisation of the Machine-Gun Corps, which would have been an asset in trench warfare, was never used in the way it was envisaged it would be. Battalion control on a tactical level was handed back to the infantry battalions for expedience. The Corps was, however, still in control of the divisional reserve and at any pause in the advance it was able to organise and co-ordinate the machine-gun activities on the whole divisional front. [20]

The reputation of the Corps reached its zenith in late 1917, with the attacks on the Hindenburg line. From March 1918 the nearly four-year old stalemate of the trenches was replaced. The carefully constructed rules that had been put together over the preceding years took a back seat and with a return to open warfare and an emphasis on direct fire. In fact, the machine-gun had become a weapon of opportunity - a phrase used in the pre-war training manuals.

The Corps was disbanded in 1922 and with almost indecent haste the guns were returned to the infantry battalions. The Corps failed to fulfil one important role that open warfare requires – co-operation and an understanding with the infantry. To achieve this both officers and men must be trained as infantrymen first and machine-gunners second. However, the lessons of massing the guns together were not totally forgotten and in the late 1930s machine-gun battalions became part of each regiment's structure.

The story of the machine-gun and the Machine-gun Corps in the First World War, mirrored that of the whole British army of the time. At first it muddled along, then grew haphazardly as guns and personnel became available, then organised itself into the most efficient force, at that time, in the world. Surely a fitting tribute to the 170,500 officers and men who served in the Corps throughout its short life. [21]

Notes

1. Major E W N Wade MC, 'From Maxim to Vickers: Some Reminiscences of an Infantry Machine-Gun Officer', *The Army Quarterly*, 1934, Vol 28.
2. Brigadier-General Sir J E Edmonds (ed), *History of the Great War: Military Operations, France and Belgium*, Macmillan and HMSO, 1927, 1915, Vol * p 58.
3. *Field Service Manual 1913: Infantry Force (Expeditionary Force)*, His Majesty's Stationery Office, p 44.
4. George Coppard, *With A Machine-gun to Cambrai*, HMSO, 1969, p 66.
5. Department of Sound Records, Baxter interview, 9346/5-2.
6. *The Register of the Victoria Cross*, This England, (publisher) 1988, p 87.
7. Colonel H A R May CBVD, *Memories of the Artists Rifles*, Howlett, p 148.
8. Lieut-Colonel G S Hutchison, *Machine-guns*, Macmillan, 1938, pp 130-131.
9. Lieut-Colonel H R Sandilands, *The 23rd Division 1914-1919*, Blackwood, 1925, p 25.
10. All Brigades of the Division had a certain number of men, varying in number from eight to sixteen per battalion.
11. Army Order, No 416, 22 October, 1915.
12. Hutchison, op cit, p 141.
13. Major R M Wright, 'Machine-Gun Tactics and Organisation', *The Army Quarterly*, January, 1921, p 292.
14. Brigadier-General Sir J Edmonds, Macmillan and HMSO, 1932, 1916 Vol*, Appendices, Appendix 21, The Somme, 1 July 1916, XIII Corps, Plan of Operations, pp 156, 160.
15. Major F W Bewsher, *The History of the 51st [Highland] Division 1914-1918*, p 104.
16. Edmonds, op cit, Vol *, p 239.
17. Ibid, p 48.
18. Lieut-Colonel J Shakespear, *The Thirty-Fourth Division 1915-1919*, Witherby, 1921, p 183.
19. Major J H Luxford, *With the machine-gunners in France and Palestine*, Whitcombe & Tombs, 1923, p 149.
20. Ibid, p 160.
21. C E Cruchley, *Machine-Gunner 1914-1918*, Baily Brothers, ND, p 15.

Too old or too bold? The removal of Sir Roger Keyes as Churchill's first Director of Combined Operations

Jeremy Langdon

Jeremy Langdon is a freelance journalist and former research assistant at the Department of War Studies, Kings' College, London.

think the Prime Minister owes me very considerable amends for my humiliating downfall and all the slanders I have suffered on his account.' [1]

So wrote an exasperated Admiral of the Fleet Sir Roger Keyes to Major-General Hastings Ismay, the War Cabinet's Deputy Secretary (Military) shortly after his removal as Director of Combined Operations on 19 October 1941. Churchill's decision to dismiss Keyes, whom he had personally appointed only fifteen months earlier in July 1940, was an acrimonious ending to a career that had been as controversial as it had been long and distinguished.

In the First World War, Keyes was Admiral de Robeck's Chief of Staff during the Dardanelles campaign and consistently urged in vain a naval forcing of the

Churchill and Keyes observing Commando exercises in Scotland, 1941. H11160

Straits. In September 1916, the youngest Rear Admiral in years, Keyes became Director of Plans at the Admiralty and as Commander of the Dover Patrol it was Keyes who orchestrated the audacious 1918 amphibious attack on Zeebrugge - the operation for which he is best remembered.

After spells as C-in-C Mediterranean and Portsmouth, Keyes entered politics in the thirties. As MP for Portsmouth North from 1934 Keyes campaigned with a small band of other Westminster realists for rearmament as Nazi Germany threatened European stability - along with Eden, Churchill and Cooper, he was one of the forty Tories who abstained during the post-Munich Commons vote in October 1938.

Eight months into the war, Keyes turned king-maker. On 7 May 1940, clad in full Admiral's garb and adorned with six rows of medals, he delivered a ferocious Commons onslaught to damn the Chamberlain government over the Norwegian fiasco and naval bungling off Trondheim. It was a speech that was described as 'a devastating attack' by Harold Nicolson who noted that:

> There is a great gasp of astonishment. It is by far the most dramatic speech that I have ever heard, and when Keyes sits down there is thunderous applause. [2]

It was an attack that some critics argue was instrumental in propelling Churchill to Downing Street only days later. Chamberlain's biographer, Keith Feiling, felt Keyes's intervention to be the 'turning point'. John Colville wrote on 8 May that 'the government is rocking'. [3] Hours later it fell. By the time it had, Churchill had already dispatched Keyes as his private liaison officer to the Belgian King Leopold - a post he filled in difficult circumstances from 10 May 1940 until the debacle of Dunkirk and the capitulation of the Belgian army eighteen days later.

Keyes, then aged sixty seven, was in the ascendant and indeed, in less than eight weeks he was apparently at the height of his power and influence. He was personally appointed by the new Prime Minister as the first Director of Combined Operations (DCO), a new position within the Whitehall defence establishment that made Keyes the Chiefs of Staff's special guru for organising raiding operations against the enemy coast. As John Colville also noted, Keyes even suggested to Churchill in November 1940 that he might become the Prime Minister's deputy to preside over the Chiefs of Staff!

Yet within fifteen months Keyes was an outcast. Shunned by Churchill, he was stripped of the DCO's title on 19 October 1941 and replaced by Lord Louis Mountbatten, then only a Captain in the Royal Navy. After an exchange of letters, Keyes was even sent a copy of the Official Secrets Act by Ismay reminding him that he must return any documents in his possession and the consequences - two years' imprisonment - of failing to do so.(The documents were still in Keyes's possession in March 1942 when they were formally demanded by the Cabinet Secretary, Edward Bridges.)

Keyes spent the rest of the war on the Commons backbenches. For a time he supported the National Savings campaign through the promotion of War Weapons Weeks and travelled around Britain by train and bus to persuade the public to invest their savings in munitions production. Annoying Churchill with his consistent Commons attacks on the direction of the war, Keyes seconded the June 1942 Vote of Censure against the Government before being created a Baron in January 1943 and sent to the House of Lords. He then undertook a tour of Australasia and the Philippines before dying from a heart condition at his Tingewick country home in Buckinghamshire on 26 December 1945. Such was the wartime rise and fall of Admiral of the Fleet Sir Roger Keyes.

But what lay behind the removal of Churchill's first Director of Combined Operations - perhaps one of the Prime Minister's strangest appointments and dismissals of the war? Was Keyes simply too old, as the press speculated and Churchill implied in his memoirs, or was he too reckless and temperamentally unsuited to the position as many of his contemporaries claimed? Had Churchill simply chosen the wrong man for the wrong job and made a gross error of personal judgement?

Churchill appointed Keyes as DCO on 17 July 1940. The move went unpublicised on the grounds of security since, as Keyes later revealed in the House of Commons, 'I was given the understanding that it might prematurely cause alarm and despondency to the enemy!' [4] He replaced General Sir Allan Bourne, Adjutant General of the Royal Marines, who had been the first 'Commander of Raiding Operations and Advisor to the Chiefs of Staff on Combined Operations'.

Churchill chose Keyes officially on the grounds of rank to lend weight to a raiding policy against the enemy coast at a time of continuous military setback. Churchill wanted Keyes to plan a series of medium scale raids using up to five thousand Commando and special service troops and the new Prime Minister wrote to Ismay that 'owing to the large scope now to be given to these operations, it is essential to have an officer of higher rank in charge...the change in no way reflects upon him (Bourne) or those associated with him.' [5] There was certainly no doubting Keyes's professional credentials for the new position. The dynamic 1914-18 hero of operations in the Dardanelles and at Zeebrugge, he appeared to possess unrivalled experience of amphibious warfare that made him a logical choice for such an appointment - particularly as Churchill was intent on instigating a 'reign of terror' against 'the whole German occupied coastline', as he put it to Ismay. [6]

However, Churchill was arguably swayed by other factors in his choice of Keyes. Both, for instance, were old friends and had been since before 1915 when they had displayed a similar desire for vigorous offensive action in the Dardanelles. That friendship had been reinforced during Keyes's diplomatic efforts on Churchill's behalf in Belgium and it was widely known that Keyes was desperate for an active command. Had nepotism, therefore, come into Churchill's decision? According to Ismay, yes - partly. Writing in 1962 the latter gave three reasons why Churchill resurrected Roger Keyes as the first DCO:

> Firstly, because he wanted to instil the idea of the offensive into everybody's mind; secondly, because he wanted to press forward with the training of Commandos and the design and production of landing-craft and all special equipment required for amphibious warfare, with a view to our ultimate return to the Continent or to landings in another part of the world; and thirdly, in order to give a job to his friend, Roger Keyes, who was badgering him day in day out.' [7]

John Colville's diary entry for 31 August 1940 also reinforces the argument that personal favouritism motivated Churchill's appointment of Keyes. According to Colville 'he has given Keyes's a job out of loyalty and affection and in so doing has much angered the younger men in the navy...On the whole I formed the impression that Sir R. Keyes's major characteristics are a well developed tendency for self-glorification'. [8]

Colville's remarks underline the fact that Keyes's appointment was not greeted with wild enthusiasm in all quarters. Admiral of the Fleet and Chief of the Naval Staff, Sir Dudley Pound, was strongly opposed and wrote:

I have seen this coming for some time. I pointed out to the PM that the employment of an officer of RK's age on a job of this kind was entirely opposed to the policy which we were urged to adopt of only employing young officers at sea. However, the PM is as pigheaded as a mule over these things and his reply was that RK was full of the flame of war etc.' [9]

The fifteen months Keyes subsequently spent as DCO were characterised by friction, squabbling and on many occasions, acrimony of which the Keyes/Pound relationship was symbolic. Any analysis of the events needs to be first judged in relation to Keyes's exact position and the nature of his duties as the DCO.

When Bourne was originally appointed 'Commander of Raiding Operations and Adviser to the Chiefs of Staff on Combined Operations' he had been informed of the scope of his powers in a Vice-Chiefs of Staff memorandum dated 17 June 1940. [10] This emphasised that, subject to directions he would receive from 'time to time' from the Chiefs of Staff, he would have 'complete discretion in the choice of objectives and the scale of operation undertaken' though he had to keep the Chiefs of Staff informed of any operations he intended to carry out. Bourne was also told that the various service departments would work out any final plans for a combined operation through the medium of the inter-service planning staff and the commander designate and that both of these would require his 'technical advice and help.' Thus Bourne's role was solely consultative and advisory.

When Keyes replaced Bourne a month later he sought to increase the powers of a directorate which, if appearing influential and grand by title, was on a practical level weak and limited in its scope for organising the type of raids Churchill wanted. As Keyes explained to Admiral Sir Andrew Cunningham, Naval C-in-C Mediterranean:

> Though I am called Director of Combined Operations, it has so far been a mis-nomer as the directive I inherited confines the responsibilities of my directive to giving technical advice on combined operations and to the training of regular troops for amphibious warfare at a training establishment at Inverary and at a number of other establishments where naval crews are trained to man the landing craft. [11]

The Royal Navy's Commander-in-Chief Mediterranean (1939-1942), Admiral Sir Andrew Cunningham. E488E

Keyes's tenure as the DCO does, then, need to be viewed against the background of his institutional crusade to reform a new defence appointment that had been created hurriedly on the enthusiastic whim of an offensively-minded new Prime Minister. Arguably, Churchill had not realised the full implications of creating the new post and how it would integrate into the mechanism of policy formulation.

A memorandum from the Vice-Chief of the Imperial General Staff, Lieutenant-General R H Haining, as early as 30 October 1940 [12] - only three months after Keyes's appointment - called for a revised directive to 'remove certain doubts which have risen regarding his responsibilities' and urged that the DCO should be given 'wider responsibilities for the training of irregular troops and a clearer definition of his responsibilities in regard to their organisation and administration'.

Keyes's DCO directive was indeed subsequently changed though not once but twice, on 14 March 1941 and then again in a Chiefs of Staff memorandum of 16 September 1941 in a manner which

was to prove unacceptable to Keyes and signal the end of his reign at Combined Operations Headquarters (COHQ), Richmond Terrace. Ostensibly, this is the reason for Keyes's dismissal - his failure to accept a new amendment to the March directive which would have dramatically weakened his already limited powers. As a comparison of the March and September directives indicates, the reduction in the scope of Keyes's powers in the space of six months was quite startling.

The March directive had been an attempt to re-define Keyes's responsibilities along the lines of Haining's memorandum. It recognised openly that the 'division of responsibility between the DCO on the one hand and the Joint Planning Staff on the other is not capable of precise definition' and that 'there must always be borderline cases which will have to be settled by *mutual consultations.*' This was an admission of the practical difficulties in clearly defining the exact limits of Keyes's powers that Churchill had not fully anticipated when creating the DCO's office.

Keyes's responsibilities 'under the general direction of the Minister of Defence and the Chiefs of Staff' were given as:

(1) The training of Special Service troops in irregular warfare and landing operations in particular.

(2) The supervision of technical training.

(3) The research and development of specialised equipment such as landing craft for opposed landings.

(4) The initiation, planning and execution of operations by Special Service troops.

(5) The provision of advice to the Chiefs of Staff as to the technical aspects of opposed landing operations including the use of carriers and landing craft

(It was also Keyes's responsibility to train naval personnel for use in carriers, landing craft and beach parties.)

Operations under the March directive would be carried out with the Joint Planning Staff with Keyes's staff preparing the part relative to the opposed landing. Subsequently, the commanders designate were meant in theory to consult Keyes and his staff when working out their plans. It was also laid down that Keyes should be present when the Chiefs of Staff were discussing the opposed landing aspect of a tabled operation. (This was a luxury Keyes was rarely to be allowed and an aspect of the directive that was flagrantly breached during the summer 1941 deliberations over Operation 'Pilgrim', the planned COHQ seizure of the Canary Islands.)

The March directive was essentially the result of an ultimatum from Keyes to Churchill over the weakness of his position. After a number of frustrated attempts to employ his newly trained Commando force, he had written to Churchill, infuriated, on 4 February 1941 asking the Prime Minister to release him from the appointment of DCO 'if it is to remain as it is at present'. The threat was reinforced on 10 February when Keyes conveyed bluntly to Churchill that: 'I cannot continue to hold the office of DCO unless I am recognised as such and given the power to be a real Director of Combined Operations.' [13]

But while Keyes agreed to the resulting directive of 14 March 1941, he could not agree to the Chiefs of Staff's subsequent directive in September which radically limited his personal powers and abolished his title. Under its terms, Keyes was to be reduced from a Director of Combined Operations to simply an 'Adviser' with no powers of initiation, command or execution of operations. Instead, by way of consolation, he was offered the chairmanship of a new inter-service committee which would study all aspects of amphibious warfare and training for combined operations. Large scale raids were transferred from the province of the DCO to the C-in-C Home Forces, with the Chiefs of Staff assuming a greater say in the conception of combined operations plans. The Chiefs of Staff completed their demolition of Keyes's office by claiming further powers to decide on the feasibility and strategy of any combined operation, while the operation commander would be responsible for all final planning - he did not even have to consult Keyes when working out details. Large scale operations on the continent would now be for the C-in-C Home Forces and appropriate naval and air Commanders-in-Chief to plan, train and execute. Finally, Keyes even lost the responsibility of supervising the development of special equipment. All in fact Keyes could salvage from the wreckage of his directorate was a concession wrung out of the Chiefs of Staff at a 'frank talk' on 27 September 1941 that he could remain in command of the Combined Training Centres such as that at Inverary. Seen overall, it was a stunning loss of power and prestige for Keyes bearing in mind the terms of his directive six months previously.

Churchill optimistically hoped that Keyes would accept this bombshell, which he termed simply 'a modification of your original directive', and even glibly suggested to Keyes that ' very large spheres of important and interesting work will be open to you as Adviser under the new arrangement ....some of the causes of friction in the past will be removed.' [14] Keyes declined to accept such a 'sweeping reduction of status' and was removed despite trying to negotiate a last ditch deal that would see him remain as a DCT - Director of Combined Training - which Churchill flatly refused.

So what had prompted Churchill to humiliate and abandon his first DCO so unceremoniously - a man he had, after all, personally appointed and backed and who he hoped would instigate the type of vigorous offensive action he so craved in some of the darkest days of the war?

As Churchill conceded in his *History of the Second World War*, this decision to ditch Keyes owed itself partly to Keyes's personality and attitude which had 'created a certain amount of friction in the service departments'. [15] The author Eric Morris goes further. Morris sees Keyes's personal failings as the chief factor in the dismissal:

> The appointment was a mistake and a major error on the part of the Prime Minister...Sir Roger Keyes was about as subtle as an air raid. He despised the Chiefs of Staff and made no secret of his views. Rather than co-ordinate, Keyes intended to empire build and to use his directorate to greater things. Indeed, one of his first steps was to divorce Combined Operations from the Admiralty and move it to lA Richmond Terrace right at the other end of Whitehall; this endeared him to few. [16]

The personality question was by no means the sole factor in Keyes's removal but there is, indeed, a great weight of evidence to suggest that Churchill should have considered more carefully the graver implications of Keyes's abrasive and forthright persona. John Colville certainly had and he noted in alarmist tones that Keyes was a 'megalomaniac' who 'carries the Zeebrugge spirit too far into his private life'. [17]

Against a background of fierce 1940/41 inter-service rivalry that had carried over from the pre-war rearmament squabbles, the new position of DCO required the trust and co-operation of Army, Royal Navy and RAF if combined operations were to be organised smoothly and effectively. Keyes's prospects for fostering a new era of inter-service harmony to implement an active raiding policy were hardly encouraging, taking into account his high ranking personal enemies, outspoken views and intimacy with Churchill.

The bitter relationship with Chief of the Naval Staff Sir Dudley Pound proved to be perhaps the greatest stumbling block for Keyes. Following his savage condemnation of the Royal Navy's performance off Norway, his relations with Pound were already severely strained before he had even assumed the DCO's office. This was not an encouraging sign given that Pound would chair the Chiefs of Staff Committee during Keyes's tenure at Richmond Terrace.

Keyes had written to Churchill - then First Lord - on 16 April 1940 to urge the adoption of his own personal plan for an assault on Trondheim using two battleships and an aircraft carrier. Churchill forced a furious Pound to examine the scheme as relations between the two men worsened. Keyes alleged that Pound was intent on 'blocking' his hopes of an active role in the conduct of Norwegian operations. An angry exchange of letters resulted in Pound retorting to Keyes that:

> I cannot imagine what caused you to suggest in your letter that I had been, as you put it, 'blocking you' and very much resent the suggestion that I should do such a thing either in your case or that of any other officer. [18]

Keyes's humiliating House of Commons condemnation of Pound and the Naval staff on 7 May 1940 set the seal on their subsequent relationship. Keyes persistently accused Pound of thwarting COHQ schemes and matters came to a head over Operation 'Workshop', Keyes's planned seizure of Pantelleria using irregular troops. As Pound wrote to Andrew Cunningham:

> Roger Keyes intrigued himself into the position of DCO in spite of the protests of the COS.....I think [that] due to RK's intrigues we are having a barging match with the PM about the status of the special service ruffians. I am sorry to say it but RK is just out for his own glorification - nothing else matters. [19]

Unsurprisingly, Keyes alleged that Pound was the prime mover in the drafting of the September 1941 directive that so dramatically reduced his personal powers.

Things were no better with the Army. Keyes had not endeared himself to senior figures in the BEF and Army establishment in his role of Churchill's private liaison officer to the Belgian King Leopold during the Phoney War and the campaign in France and Belgium in May 1940. His later defence of Leopold after the Belgian surrender on 28 May and the debacle at Dunkirk called him to challenge the 'official' version of events in France and Belgium which the BEF Commander, Gort, was about to publish on the campaign - particularly 'the allegation that disaster in France had stemmed from a cowardly and sudden Belgian capitulation which had

Chief of the Naval Staff (1939-1943), Admiral of the Fleet Sir Dudley Pound. A20791

exposed the BEF's left flank and necessitated a withdrawal to the coast (this spurious charge was finally put to rest by Keyes's son in his excellent study of the campaign in Belgium and the actions of King Leopold). [20]

Matters were not helped by Keyes's libel action against the *Daily Mirror* after that paper had criticised Leopold (the 'rat king') and the Admiral in a vitriolic leader of 30 May 1940. Keyes's crusade to expose the failings of the BEF rumbled on through the months of his tenure at COHQ, souring his relations with senior military men and finally exposing an embarrassing cover up - the British Army's attempt to blame Belgium for events culminating at Dunkirk. Lieutenant-General Henry Pownall, Vice-Chief of the Imperial General Staff in 1941, seemed to speak for many in the Army when writing scornfully of Keyes's involvement with the formulation of Operation 'Pilgrim':

> Keyes continually criticises the strategical aspect of the whole thing and this is no business of his whatsoever. But Winston put him in and it's the devil of a job to get him

out. Not that Winston has any faith in him I'm sure. [21]

A further obstacle was the Army's deep cynicism about the independent Commando units Keyes was training. The belief that Keyes's Commandos should remain under Army and not COHQ control was a point that rankled with many generals like Alan Brooke, the C-in-C Home Forces. Brooke fought not only to reduce the independence of Keyes and his Commandos but also to transfer combined operations to the remit of his own office. He wrote in September 1941 after three days with Keyes at the Combined Operations Training Centre at Inverary that:

> The whole of my visit to Roger Keyes was an attempt on his part to try and convince me that our Commando policy was right. He failed to do so and I remained convinced until the end of the war that the Commandos should never have been divorced from the army in the way they were. [22]

Keyes's relationships with the two Chiefs of Air Staff who sat during his tenure as DCO, Newall and his replacement in September 1940, Portal, were likewise conducted against the background of his consistent public criticism of the Air Ministry and the RAF's reluctance to give the Admiralty independent control of the Fleet Air Arm and Coastal Command.

In a letter to Churchill on 12 February 1940, for instance, Keyes had referred scathingly to a 'self-centred Air Ministry who have never tried to understand naval requirements and have impeded the development of Naval aviation most damnably during the last twenty years with the result that the Germans can quite fairly claim that they dominate the air over the North Sea.' He finished his outburst by despairing of how 'Fighter and Bomber Commands have neglected Coastal Command interests so shockingly.' [23] Keyes carried his prejudices against the Air Ministry into his work as the DCO. Attempting to secure aircraft for parachute trainees, he complained to Ismay that 'the Air Ministry puts every obstacle in the way of carrying them overseas'. [24]

However, while Churchill should have realised the personal antagonisms that Keyes's appointment aroused, he certainly did not remove Keyes because he had failed in his duties. The great irony of Keyes's dismissal is that he *had* actually made a success of his new job. He had organised the 'thoroughly equipped raiding units' that Churchill had initially envisaged in June 1940 would take the war back to the Germans and he would doubtless have developed the 'reign of terror' down the enemy coast with raids that Churchill hoped would leave 'a trail of German corpses behind them'. Indeed, from inheriting in July 1940 no troop - or tank - carrying ships, no specialised aircraft, only four tank-carrying landing craft and only one thousand two hundred and fifty Commando and independent troops, Keyes had organised five thousand men into ten well trained Commandos by the time of his dismissal fifteen months later and in addition had developed the landing craft and troopships which would later play such a crucial role on the Normandy beaches. It was not Keyes's fault that for the vast majority of his time as DCO his Commandos went unused.

Ten days after Keyes had taken over as the DCO, Churchill wrote to him on 27 July 1940 urging him to 'Let me have at your earliest convenience...three or four proposals for medium sized action (i.e. between five and ten thousand men). I certainly think we should be acting in September or October.' [25] The early omens for combined operations, with the personal backing and encouragement of Churchill, seemed very promising but what followed underlined the weakness of Keyes's personal position and that of COHQ within Whitehall. When taking into account the period of near continuous military defeat and setback endured by Britain in 1940/41, the catalogue of frustrations suffered by COHQ in their attempts to initiate offensive action makes very curious reading.

In August 1940, Churchill asked Keyes how many men he could produce to aid the capture of Dakar - Operation 'Menace'. Despite offering 2,350 men, who Keyes felt could be properly equipped in only 48 hours, Churchill chose to ignore the offer. Churchill also chose to ignore the fact that Landriau, the French Naval Commander-in-Chief at Dakar, had served under Keyes at Dover and had been decorated on Keyes's recommendation, prompting optimism at COHQ that Landriau would come to terms without bloodshed. Keyes's men and advice shunned, Dakar turned out to be a fiasco and Operation 'Menace' was aborted.

Further frustrations followed. On 9 September l940 all Keyes's Commandos were placed under the C-in-C Home Forces and not returned to COHQ control until early December, interrupting for two months their specialised training at Inverary. Meanwhile, the force of 2,500 Commandos Keyes had assembled to capture the Mediterranean island of Pantelleria - Operation 'Workshop' – was approved by the Chiefs of Staff on 2 November and scheduled to leave on

14 December with Keyes commanding. The date of departure was then postponed twice before the operation was finally cancelled on the eve of sailing on 30 January. The reason given by the Chiefs of Staff was the arrival of German dive bombers in Sicily though, ironically, these planes had forestalled Keyes's force only because of the repeated delays in its departure! This force was then split up and sent to the Middle East via the long Cape route - against Keyes's advice - in the three best transport ships available. Here, in Keyes's words, ' they were several times on the point of carrying out enterprises only to be stopped at the last moment and then frittered away and dispersed'. [26]

Undeterred, Keyes organised and trained another force of six thousand men for the capture of the Canary Islands - Operation 'Pilgrim' - an amalgamation of previous COHQ plans to capture the Azores (Operation 'Thruster'), Madeira ('Springboard') and the Canaries and Cape Verdes ('Puma'). This force was then taken by the Chiefs of Staff and placed under the command of two relatively inexperienced Joint Commanders, Rear Admiral Hamilton and Major-General Alexander. The result was the men and ships went unused for four months and once again German reinforcements forestalled the operation. Despite Keyes's protestations, this second force and a number of their ships were sent off to Sierra Leone, 1300 miles beyond their original objective, which in Keyes's words 'deprived us of the means of carrying out large scale raiding operations from this country'.

In short, when taking into account that other projected operations in the Channel Islands, Casablanca and Norway were discussed but never approved, the only attack of any note carried out by Keyes's Commandos during his reign as DCO was the first raid on the Lofoten Islands on 3 March 1941. (This was a minor unopposed expedition to destroy fishing installations off the north Norwegian coast and deny the German Army vitamin pills which were manufactured from Norwegian fish oil.)

This unhappy list of operational abortions and planning problems chiefly explains the friction and acrimony that characterised Keyes's fifteen months at Richmond Terrace. Keyes bombarded Churchill, Ismay and Eden with a stream of letters pointing out what he considered the barriers to the successful prosecution of combined operations. As early as 27 August 1940 he wrote despairingly to Ismay that:

It is not easy to get on with the war. I haven't bothered the PM again as there is really nothing he can do unless he thinks offensively

and gets two or three offensive spirits free from everlasting committees to help him to do so. [27]

On 1 February 1941 he sent Churchill a long letter that turned into a tirade against the mechanism of policy formulation which saw combined operations plans such as 'Workshop' continually sabotaged by the objections and doubts of the Naval Staff:

Everyone is sick to death with the Naval Staff...it is difficult to justify their retention in office after their past record. The ability of a few comparatively junior officers - who have no practical experience in war and have nothing but their fears to guide them - to stifle offensive efforts so deplorably is ever more inexplicable. [28]

Interestingly, Keyes actually attributes his downfall in surviving papers and letters principally to one naval officer, Captain L E H Maund. (Maund was later made the scapegoat for the sinking of HMS *Ark Royal* in November 1941 and court martialled for the carrier's loss off Gibraltar.)

Before commanding *Ark Royal* and, indeed before being appointed the Naval Chief of Staff for Narvik Operations in April 1940, Maund had been instrumental in the establishment of the Inter-Service Training and Development Centre at Eastney - the early forerunner of COHQ. He had then become Deputy Director to General Bourne in June 1940, becoming the acknowledged naval authority on combined operations.

Admiral Sir James Somerville, Commander 'H' Force (left) and Captain L E H Maund (right) on the flight deck of HMS *Ark Royal*. H11167

When Keyes replaced Bourne in July, Maund was removed to landing craft development at the Admiralty from where he drafted an anonymous memorandum of 11 December 1940, circulated while Keyes was in Scotland.

This suggested the COHQ organisation was flawed and that the Admiralty, who controlled both ships and personnel at Inverary, and the military, who controlled Keyes's men, could well do without the interposition of a DCO between Inverary and the two service departments. Maund attacked an 'unsound' chain of command and, as Keyes later described, suggested 'that my Directorate was redundant and should be abolished'.

Keyes was convinced that Maund was the chief plotter in a naval conspiracy to remove him and speculated, after his fall, that Maund had organised an intrigue against him involving other leading naval officers at Gibraltar from where Maund commanded the *Ark Royal*.

This was correct up to a point. There was undoubtedly exasperation with Keyes at Gibraltar, where a number of senior naval figures felt Keyes to be too old, too reckless, too out of date and friendly with Churchill to the point that he had held up the attack on the Dodecanese Islands by pestering the Prime Minister with Operation 'Workshop'. Indeed, from this dissatisfaction with Keyes hatched a conspiracy to have him removed. However, Keyes's main detractor was not a mere Captain. Instead, in August 1941, three leading Mediterranean based Admirals dispatched a messenger to London to urge Churchill that Keyes should be replaced.

The courier was Wing Commander Archibald James, the First Secretary at the British Embassy in Madrid, who regularly liaised with high ranking naval officers at Gibraltar. As unpublished memoirs held by his family now confirm, James was begged and authorised to go to London by Admirals Somerville, North and Cunningham as a 'responsible freelance' to make the 'earliest possible and most urgent representation through whatever channel' to persuade Churchill that Keyes was complicating the naval chain of command - principally by his high rank which was superior to each of theirs. James describes an undated meeting at North's residence in Gibraltar in which both North and Somerville were present. Cunningham was not present but had sent a Commodore to act as his personal representative. According to James's memoirs:

> They all personally liked and admired Roger but felt that he was too old, too out of date

Wing Commander Archibald James, First Secretary at the British Embassy at Madrid in 1941. Reproduced by kind permission of Hugh and Billy James.

and too reckless for the job....further objections were that besides being Winston's personal friend, to have an Admiral of the Fleet loose in the Med. could hopelessly complicate their tasks. [29]

The James mission to London is still shrouded in some mystery. The precise date, for instance, is not given in his memoir manuscript. What is clear, however, is that James did not report to Churchill directly but chose to disclose his information to General Ismay whom he knew personally. Keyes later accused Ismay of relating the details of his meeting with James to Churchill, complaining 'Don't you think you might have warned me of this damned intrigue and passing on what you must have known were lies?' Ismay replied with a categorical assurance that he did not pass on 'tittle tattle' to the Prime Minister. [30]

However, what the James mission does

confirm is Keyes's erroneous obsession with making Captain L E H Maund the chief culprit for his fall. Clearly his main detractors were much more distinguished and influential. Mrs Constance Maund, the widow of the *Ark Royal* Captain - recently interviewed by the author - pours scorn on the idea that her husband could have possibly influenced the downfall of Keyes, principally on the grounds that he was only a captain at the time and was 'hardly in a position to influence how the navy thought, still less how Churchill acted'. [31] Moreover, none of her late husband's personal correspondence hints at any overt hostility to Keyes. Maund may certainly have resented Keyes for usurping him as the acknowledged naval expert on combined operations and been incensed by Keyes's violent criticism of naval operations off Norway in 1940, in which Maund played a leading role. However, Keyes's contention that Maund then hatched a plot to remove him are unfounded.

Two important naval fears about Sir Roger Keyes appear to have prompted the James mission - his rank and his recklessness. Somerville had urged James to convey to Churchill that 'brave men's lives will be thrown away on some hare-brained scheme'. [32] Indeed, as Somerville's comments suggest, there is no doubt that leading Admiralty figures were deeply alarmed about the feasibility of some of Keyes's major projects.

The saga over Operation 'Workshop', the plan to capture and garrison Pantelleria - which Churchill enthusiastically backed and felt would have an 'electrifying effect' - is a good case in point. Dudley Pound wrote to Andrew Cunningham for example in December 1940 that:

> The 'Workshop' plan started the wrong end as RK put up the suggestion without having made any investigation of it whatsoever. The next step was that a half baked plan was put before the COS and of course when we criticised it, it was insinuated that we were trying to kill it and to do nothing. As you will realise as soon as you have anything to do with him, RK is not capable of making out a plan and you would certainly be very unwise to allow him to do so. [33]

Having asked to command the 'Workshop' operation, Keyes admitted that he had never even considered having to produce a detailed plan once Churchill had given him the go ahead to lead it. He felt that having been given a free hand to organise a much larger and hazardous attack on Zeebrugge in 1918, he was excused having to satisfy 'junior staff officers' with fine details. [34]

But Pound was not alone in questioning the planning aspects of 'Workshop. Cunningham himself wrote bluntly to Keyes that 'Workshop' had been impractical on the grounds of supply:

> I am glad it did not take place. I think it would have been a disaster. We are having enough difficulty at the moment in supplying Malta without having to supply an island one hundred and fifty miles beyond. [35]

If Keyes was as reckless as Somerville, Pound and Cunningham thought there was another main factor which also aroused controversy and bitterness as the James memoirs indicate - his rank. Subordinate in formal position to the Chiefs of Staff, Ismay and the inter-service planners with whom he had to liaise, the great paradox of Keyes's position was that he personally outranked many of his 'superiors' at the same time - as he did Admirals North, Cunningham and Somerville. The friction that this situation was creating was emphasised by a Chiefs of Staff paper in November 1940 which stated that:

> The main difficulty is, of course, that the DCO is an Admiral of the Fleet and as DCO can hardly be subordinate to JPS (Joint Planning Committee)....an officer of such exalted rank should not hold this position and have direct access to the Chiefs of Staff on planning matters.... [36]

Churchill later wrote to Keyes prior to his dismissal that ' Your very high rank and personal association with me cause embarrassment and friction' and, indeed, Keyes's successor in October 1941, Mountbatten - a naval Captain - was chosen, according to Ismay, partly on the grounds that there was considered to be less likelihood of rows between the Chiefs of Staff and Combined Operations if the head of the latter was a relatively junior officer. [37]

Neither did Keyes benefit from the fact that after March 1941, Churchill delegated Ismay to liaise with him on combined operations matters. This was surprising given that Churchill had personally appointed Keyes and that Keyes had initially been a regular Chequers guest and confidant of the Prime Minister after being appointed DCO. The result was that Churchill only saw Keyes twice personally from June 1941 until his dismissal, announced by letter on 4 October. Both meetings were very brief and it seems strange, despite Churchill's exhausting schedule, that Keyes should be denied

Colonel Leslie Hollis (left), Assistant Secretary (Military) to the War Cabinet and Chiefs of Staff Committee on board HMS *Prince of Wales*, August 1941. H12793

Churchill's personal ear in a period coinciding with lengthy deliberations over Operation 'Pilgrim'. Churchill's decision to use Ismay as an intermediary arguably indicates that he had begun to reconsider Keyes's appointment long before he decided to replace him - at least by the spring of 1941.

Keyes seems to have trusted Ismay to give him a favourable hearing in the Chiefs of Staff Committee and with the Prime Minister. Indeed, on his replacement by Mountbatten, Keyes thanked Ismay warmly in a letter for his help over the 'difficult' months of his directorate. Yet there seems to be a good deal of evidence that Ismay was not the help that Keyes assumed he was. For instance, Ismay surprisingly told Keyes nothing of his meeting with James and did not always brief Churchill fully on COHQ plans. In his memoirs, Ismay failed to see why Keyes had been acclaimed for his May 1940 outburst over Norway and following Keyes's dismissal, he steadfastly refused to circulate to the Prime Minister a paper Keyes had drafted on the use of amphibious power in the Mediterranean. As Ismay dismissively wrote to Edward Bridges, Churchill's Cabinet Secretary on 9 December 1941:

> I should not have thought that anybody, however distinguished his past, had a right to demand that his paper should be circulated to the Minister of Defence and the War Cabinet.

> If that precedent were once established we should find ourselves in Queer Street! [38]

In fact, Ismay's true feelings about Keyes as the DCO were best summed up after the war:

> Keyes was as tactless as he could have been...he had, before his appointment, drifted around Whitehall saying that the Chiefs of Staff were a bunch of lily livered so-and-sos and seemed to imagine that as Director of Combined Operations he was going to have the right of planning and leading expeditions all over the world....the crash was bound to come. [39]

The crash finally came in unusual circumstances in the early hours of 4 October 1941 in a dramatic interview involving neither Ismay, Pound, Maund nor Keyes. Instead, Keyes's dismissal was the result of a meeting between Churchill and Ismay's deputy, Colonel Leslie Hollis, who had assumed Ismay's duties while he was away in Moscow with Lord Beaverbrook and Averell Harriman on a mission to organise military aid for Stalin. The scene was the Cabinet room at 10 Downing Street. According to the account in Hollis's wartime memoirs, it was he who persuaded Churchill to remove Keyes because of the pressure being exerted on the Chiefs of Staff. As Hollis told Churchill:

> He is taking up far too much of the Chiefs of Staff time. His plans aren't feasible, yet he is continually bombarding them with new suggestions for landings, raids and attacks on remote, unimportant places when they have more than enough to do in coping with their own work. Then, when his plans are turned down, as they invariably are, they all have to be reconsidered because he has your ear...and he refuses to take "No" for an answer. [40]

The Hollis account has never been challenged nor indeed denied - certainly not by Keyes's biographer Cecil Aspinall-Oglander nor Churchill in his *History of the Second World War*, neither of whom mention it. Yet if it is to be believed, Churchill essentially dismissed Keyes on the basis of a ten minute meeting on the recommendation of his War Cabinet's Senior Assistant Military Secretary - a surprising manner in which to decide to remove such a high-ranking officer and personal friend whom Churchill had personally appointed.

Even more bizarre, according to Leasor, is how, having had the dismissal letter drafted and signed there and then, Churchill gave it to Hollis to post which he promptly did. Leasor then records that Churchill frantically telephoned Hollis four hours later pleading, 'you didn't despatch that letter, I hope.... I feel that we have been much too hard, much too hard. I don't want it to go'. [41]

In conclusion, the downfall of Admiral of the Fleet and DCO Sir Roger Keyes is passed over rather too quickly and uncontroversially by Churchill in Volume III of his *History of the Second World War*. According to Churchill it was the simple result of age - as deduced by Fleet Street at the time - and personality factors:

> Roger Keyes had now reached the age of seventy. He had performed invaluable service in building up the commandos and in pressing forward the design and construction of naval craft. His rank of Admiral of the Fleet and strong personality had created a certain amount of friction in the Service departments, and I reached the conclusion with much regret on personal grounds that the appointment of a new and young figure at the head of the overseas organisation would be in the public interest. [42]

Keyes, who reached the age of sixty-nine on the very day he was dismissed, conceded in the House of Commons five weeks after his fall that this was 'a young men's war'. Yet his fall also asks fundamental questions about Churchill's leadership and judgement. It can be argued that a new Prime Minister foolishly appointed a high ranking intimate personal friend to a new defence directorate that was bound to be viewed suspiciously and jealously by the services and Chiefs of Staff. Such had been Churchill's haste to initiate a raiding policy and create a DCO, that the wider implications on policy formulation had been ignored - hence the changing of Keyes's directive twice and the complications caused by his high rank. To make matters worse, Keyes, despite an illustrious background in amphibious operations, was personally unsuited to the role and had influential enemies in all three Services and particularly poor relations with the Chief of the Naval Staff, Sir Dudley Pound.

Keyes's reign as Director of Combined Operations was consequently clouded by friction and squabbling which obscured the valuable work he undoubtedly did accomplish to organise the Commando units that Mountbatten inherited. The Commando 'reign of terror' never materialised - indeed partly because Churchill initially forbade pinprick combined operations in home waters for fear of 'working all these coasts up against us' as he put it to Eden in July 1940. [43]

Amidst all the bickering, only one raid of any note was mounted, on the Lofoten Islands, and even this saw argument between Keyes and the C-in-C Home Fleet about the use of destroyers for bombardment. Countless other COHQ plans were mangled by the institutional problems of planning and co-ordination that Churchill had failed to anticipate. Keyes was unable to prevent the sabotage of these plans because of the weakness of his position and the fact that he was bypassed. For example, Churchill flagrantly breached Keyes's March directive by removing him from Chiefs of Staff deliberations concerning Operation 'Pilgrim'. The furore that followed the botched dress rehearsal for 'Pilgrim', Exercise 'Leapfrog' at Scapa Flow on 10 August 1941, ignored the fact that Keyes had objected to its taking place. The chaos at Scapa underlined the confusion in the control of combined operations. The Prime Minister even asked the C-in-C Home Forces, General Brooke, to set up a feasibility study for a cross-channel raid for the spring of 1942, a clear snub to Keyes and all at COHQ, Richmond Terrace.

Rumours of naval discontent with Keyes in Gibraltar reached Whitehall as a result of Wing

Commander Archibald James's August 1941 mission that was sponsored by a trio of leading Admirals. James conveyed criticism of Keyes's age, his rank, the recklessness of his plans and his intimacy with the Prime Minister. Combined with the consistent hostility to Keyes of Chief of the Naval Staff Sir Dudley Pound, Churchill was forced to take action. He had it seemed, already realised his mistake and sent Keyes to a political 'Coventry', keeping him at arm's length by delegating General Ismay to act as an intermediary - a move that further isolated and undermined Keyes. Under pressure to back or sack the DCO, Churchill eventually relied on the instant judgement of the Senior Military Assistant Secretary to the War Cabinet, Colonel Hollis, to convince himself that removing Keyes was the only course open - even then suffering an emotional last minute change of heart once the dismissal letter had been sent.

Ultimately the saga of Sir Roger Keyes as DCO illuminates Churchill's own immaturity as a military leader and his own reckless desire to wage war without fully appreciating the implications of personal whims and personal appointments. As Barrie Pitt noted, 'How fortunate we have been that such wise, firm, coldly logical strategists were in a position to restrain the silly, boyish determination of people like Keyes and Churchill, who simply wanted to go off and win the war by attacking the enemy'. [44]

The Prime Minister's treatment of Keyes was, indeed, rather shabby. After the war, Ismay was invited to annotate draft chapters of Churchill's *History of the Second World War*. Asked for his reflections on the cancellation of Operation 'Workshop' on 18 January 1941, Ismay sagely reminded Churchill that:

> Admiral Keyes was not present at the meeting but heard the result of it in London and arrived at Ditchley just before dinner that night in order to argue the matter with you. You would not see him but we gave him a drink and sent him back to London! [45]

Notes

1. PRO/DEFE 2/698,14 November 1941.
2. N Nicolson (ed), *Harold Nicolson Diaries and Letters 1939-45*, London, 1967; Fontana paperback, 1970, p 136.
3. Keith Feiling, *Life of Neville Chamberlain*, London 1946, and John Colville, *The Fringes of Power Volume 1 1939 - October 1941*, London, 1986. Sceptre paperback, p 136.
4. *Hansard*, 25 November 1941.
5. PRO/DEFE 2/ 698.
6. C Aspinall-Oglander, *Roger Keyes*, London 1951, p 380. Churchill to Ismay, 6 June 1940.
7. Liddell Hart Centre for Military Archives(LHCMA), Ismay Papers, IV/MOU/ 34a. Ismay to Cdr R Boulsfield, 15 November 1962.
8. Colville, p 276.
9. Cunningham Papers, British Library MS 52561, Pound to Cunningham, 12 December 1940.
10. PRO/AIR8/1044, C.O.S(40)468, 17 June 1940.
11. British Library MS 52569, 13 December 1940.

12. PRO/AIR/8/1044, C.O.S (40) 889.
13. PRO/DEFE 2/698.
14. PRO/DEFE 2/6981, Churchill to Keyes, 30 September 1941.
15. W S Churchill, *History of the Second World War, Volume III The Grand Alliance*, London, 1950, p 480.
16. Eric Morris, *Churchill's Private Armies*, London, 1986, p 127-129.
17. Colville, p 351 and 378.
18. Pound Papers, DUPO 3/6, Churchill College, Cambridge. Pound to Keyes, 29 April 1940.
19. British Library MS52561, Pound to Cunningham, l5 December 1940.
20. Roger Keyes, *Outrageous Fortune - The Tragedy of Leopold III of the Belgians 1901-1941*, London, 1984.
21. Brian Bond (ed), *Chief of Staff - The Diaries of Lt. General Sir Henry Pownall, Vol I 1933-40*, London, 1973, pp 43-44.
22. (LHCMA) Alanbrooke Papers, Notes on My Life, (September 1941).
23. PRO/ADM205/6.
24. PRO/DEFE 2/6981, Keyes to Ismay, 27 August 1940.
25. PRO/DEFE 2/698.
26. Ibid.

27. Ibid.
28. Ibid.
29. From the unpublished James memoirs.
30. (LHCMA), lsmay Papers, 'IV/Keyes'. Keyes to Ismay, 14 November 1941 and Ismay to Keyes, 17 November 1941.
31. Letter to the author, 25 July 1992.
32. James memoirs.
33. British Library MS 52561, Pound to Cunningham, 12 December 1940.
34. PRO/DEFE 2/698, 'History of Workshop'.
35. Keyes Papers, British Library MS, 'Keyes 13/20', Cunningham to Keyes, 4 March 1941.
36. PRO/AIR/8/1044, Chiefs of Staff 376th meeting memo, 6 November 1940.
37. Ismay to Boulsfield, qv.
38. (LHCMA), Ismay Papers, 'IV/Keyes'.
39. Ismay to Boulsfield,qv.
40. James Leasor, *War at the Top - The Experiences of General Sir Leslie Hollis KCB KBE*, London, 1959, p123.
41. Ibid.
42. W S Churchill, op cit, p 480.
43. Morris, p 130.

44. Barrie Pitt, *Zeebrugge*, Cassell, London, 1958, p 221.
45. (LHCMA), Ismay Papers, 'II/3/132/2b'.

Further reading

Lord Ismay, *The Memoirs of Lord Ismay*, London, 1960.
R Lamb, *Churchill as War Leader - Right or Wrong*, London, 1991.
N Nicholson (ed), *Harold Nicholson Diaries and Letters*, London, 1967.
P Ziegler, *Mountbatten*, Collins, London and New York, 1985.

Acknowledgements

Thanks are due to Mrs Constance Maund for letting me consult her late husband's correspondence. Hugh and Billy James very kindly offered me access to their father's unpublished memoirs while Professor Brian Bond, Peter Simkins and Suzanne Bardgett offered sensible and constructive criticisms on the text.

Eton and the First World War

Andrew Robinson

My losses in the war are heart-rending: it would seem as if the very pick and best of all are marked for death, and the blows come so steadily.... How the nation is to recover in the next generation I can't see at all, since the fittest do not survive...

Henry Edward Luxmoore, Eton, 22 December 1917.

Gott Strafe Harrow.

Text of a telegram sent from Abbeville to the editor of the Eton College Chronicle, *June 1915.*

Eton College, nearly five centuries old, with more than a thousand boys in its Houses, was empty at the outbreak of the First World War, on holiday after a particularly sunlit Summer term. There exists a photograph showing the entire school gathered round its Head Master and King George V before the chapel steps in the summer of 1913, cheering the news that the king, in honour of the arrival of his third son, Prince Henry, to board at Eton, had requested a whole week's extra holiday. Ironically, all the faces are peering skywards; they are looking at a passing airship. A thousand cheering boys. In the next five years, more than that number, some 1,157, would be killed.

Perhaps the sense of the destruction of a generation given by the retired house master, Luxmoore, above is statistically exaggerated [1], but it must have felt like it in the context of such a concentration of youth. Young men left the school, leaving their brothers, cousins and friends behind them. They left for the most part to become a portion of one of the Great War's most perishable elements: its subalterns. In a few years the brothers, cousins and friends were to join them.

It has seemed right to start with the two quotations, the first explained above, the second, adopting a tone with an acute focus on sporting rivalries and concomitant lack of sensitivity displaying a perhaps oafish contribution (later apologised for to Harrow) to Eton's summer feast of pageantry, cricket and aquatics, the Fourth of June. [2] A historian of the public school ethos [3] has discussed at some length the influence of that ethos on the very excitement of 1914, and blamed it for the persistence of such a mood, in spite of realities, for so long and to such destructive effect. But a discussion of a

Andrew Robinson is a master at Eton College.

Eton College Officer Training Corps performing rifle drill, 1909.
Reproduced by permission of the Provost and Fellows of Eton College.

school at war might take into account not just that particular ethos, but a mixture - a mixture of doomed enthusiasm with the anguish also expressed above, admittedly by the much older man who saw the lives of his Old Boys thrown away. In giving an account of a public school at war, this article seeks to show both these spirits abroad.

Etonians returning to school in September 1914 found their numbers significantly reduced, especially among the older boys. More than fifty had gone straight from Corps camp - along with their Adjutant - to regiment. [4] Survivors talk of a mood in which everyone wanted to join up as soon as possible. Quite a number of the younger masters disappeared as well, their places taken, it seemed to some, by some curious specimens:

The turmoil of war dims everything else. The boys flock prematurely to the Front, and House Masters will soon be in a tight corner. Strange supplementary dons take Fourth Forms whose masters have gone to the Front, and two dozen Belgian boys fraternise amicably with ours and go into school in knicker-bockers... [5]

One of the 'strange supplementary dons' - university figures, unused to the style of lesson suitable to the fourteen-year old mind, employed at Eton during the war - was Aldous Huxley. The introduction of Belgian refugees, though conducted in an atmosphere of cordial goodwill and birthday telegrams to King Albert of the Belgians, whose son was among the new boarders, reflected, too, a need to keep the numbers up.

The arrival of refugees and the first news of casualties - nine days after the beginning of the school year, the first list of the Etonian war dead was published in the School *Chronicle* - must have brought events in France and Flanders closer to boys at Eton. Perhaps contact could be a little rarefied. A talk was given by the aged Belgian diplomat Prince Alfonse de Chimay, who recounted his experience of Belgium under the Germans - 'the death of chivalry'- and also told his young audience, who may by this time have seen recruiting posters on the subject of Belgian neutrality, that, 'As a young attaché, in response to a request from his ambassador, he had received from Lord Palmerston's lips the assurance of England's undying loyalty to her word...' [6]

The presence of Belgians and distinguished outside speakers - Austen Chamberlain came to speak on 'some broader aspects of the war' in December 1914 - cannot have pressed the realities of war on the school so forcibly as the mounting list of its dead. A section, 'Etona Non Immemor' with a Roll of the latest dead appeared in the *Chronicle*, along with a list of those Etonians fighting. There were 736 combatant by the New Year in 1915, and 1,400 a year later, with 160 already killed. Those at the Front were remembered in a regular service of intercession in the School Chapel:

> The Bell is not allowed (and the lights are kept down) so it is rather difficult not to be late for it. Chapel is generally pretty well filled...we have a psalm or a hymn sung and a litany of sorts and the names of the fallen in the week... [7]

The lists of the dead were supplemented by obituary notices, not infrequently reporting the apparent manner of death. John Scudamore, a lieutenant in the King's Royal Rifle Corps, who had left in 1914 and was killed at Loos in 1915, aged 19, on September 25 1915:

> He was killed instantaneously leading his men to the assault, and had all but cut his way through the German wire. The fact that he was well in front of his men shows the gallantry with which he went forward. [8]

Peter Parker has written of the influence of the spirit of organised games on the attitude of public schoolboys to war in 1914-18, and certainly it is present in the extract above. Less than eighteen months earlier, Scudamore had been playing cricket at Eton. In that same year Logie Leggatt, an Old Etonian King's Scholar also serving in the

King's Royal Rifle Corps, had written from France of the 'alarming increase in the girth of the whole Division since they entered upon this sedentary life which passes in these degenerate days.' He called on his old school friends to send football jerseys and shorts to the Front so that a programme of sports could be arranged.

Keep-fit programmes were not the only use for which surplus sporting equipment might be thought valuable. A house master asked boys to send him spare pairs of gloves they had to play 'Eton Fives' since:

> Waste soft leather is used by the Ladies' Territorial Committee to make windproof undercoats for our soldiers and sailors. Incidentally, this work kept 60 women employed all through last winter at a good living wage. [9]

When on OTC activities, boys used football rattles to simulate machine gun fire. A recruiting poster for the Public Schools Battalion [10] exhorting its viewers 'Come on boys! Fill the ranks' shows a *Boys' Own* hero astride a trench, a pile of captured *pickelhaube* at his feet. The message of such a poster to those reared on games was clear; it was matched by efforts to persuade working class men to follow their footballing heroes to the Front. But it must be an error to think this the only way in which boys thought about the war:

> My inside is turned still after that beastly gas; it really is more than the limit...I have seen Ypres a roaring mass of flames from end to end, a most extraordinary, magnificent sight; I also passed through the place at 3 a.m., when there was absolute desolation - the fire burnt out, and not a living soul to be seen...I have also seen that place of despair known as Hill 60.

This, a 'letter from an old Colleger at the Front', appeared in the College *Chronicle*, the same issue as that which bore the appeals for footballs for the Front. By the autumn of 1915 the school had been saddened by the deaths of two masters, themselves Old Etonians, George Fletcher and Dick Durnford. [11] The Chronicle began to record accounts of Etonians' recounting their war experiences to those still at school. They had heard a curious lecture on 'Trench warfare' from an Irish Guards officer seemingly on the importance of wire:

> Wire is of paramount importance, and the

Recruiting poster for the Public Schools Brigade, POS204.

place it occupies in the minds of those at the Front is enormous. They literally live in, for and by wire. As a subject for conversation it entirely supplants anything else, and it is the one thing which can never be neglected without disaster. The reputation of a regiment at the Front depends as much on the state in which it keeps wire and its parapet and the general state of its trench as it does on its actual performances in action. [12]

But there was also a lecture from Captain E H Impey: [13]

This isn't war. I've been fired on with a working party, been shelled coming up and down the communicating trenches...but I haven't been able to hit back. We sit and wait

for death from a hidden Hun who uses a large 'bang' stick, and we do the same... [14]

In the Autumn of 1915 too, the boys would have heard John Christie, a dilettantish science master (later the founder of Glyndebourne Opera),lecture on his experiences serving with the Rifle Corps, though his letters to a fellow master from Loos, riddled with bloody vignettes and Eton gossip, were labelled 'not for publication' by their recipient.

Boys too young to fight were eager to assist with fund-raising efforts. The first project was to clothe the arriving Belgian boys (21 of them); this was then extended to raise the funds for two field ambulances for the French. £400 was raised, £375 for the vehicles, and £3 for suitably inscribed silver plates to be fitted to them. The money came from the boys, from the Head Master, and from £170 raised at a School concert at which Dame Clara Butt had sung 'Land of Hope and Glory.'

The school Debating Society discussed topics of immediate interest: 'whether the annihilation of Prussia was desirable', 'whether it would be to the advantage of Italy to enter the War on the side of the Allies at once' (also carried) and, interestingly, 'whether arbitration will take the place of war after the present crisis'.

The discussion of the third debate given here is significant, in that it is reported that the Headmaster, Edward Lyttelton, was praised for an excellent speech on 'the absurdity of modern war'. [15] Lyttelton's views were soon to attract a wider and more hostile audience. So far as sermons at school went, they would seem to have been filled with a sense of duty and patriotism. A visiting preacher on 22 October 1914 had spoken on the text 'Friend, how camest thou in hither not having a wedding garment?' reminding his audience of the anniversaries of Edgehill, Trafalgar and Agincourt which fell that week. A few months later the fiery bishop of Pretoria, Michael Furse, arrived:

almost straight from the Front and foaming at the mouth. He preached on Whitsunday and stirred us all - some boys shocked by mention of 'cigarettes' in the pulpit. He says nothing in his experience is so like the early Church as the front-line army... [16]

Lyttelton's line, at least when he was away from his school, was markedly different. He had perhaps not a towering intellect, being known from his passion for outdoor games as 'The Brown Man'. But he did have

General Gough addressing pupils.
Reproduced by permission of the Provost and Fellows of Eton College.

certain views on attitudes to the war which, when he put them into a sermon delivered at St Margaret's Church, Westminster, in Holy Week 1915 were to earn him national notoriety.

Even from a distant perspective, Lyttelton's views seem controversial. [17] He said that 'it was his view that if we were going to act as a Christian nation we were bound to apply the principle of Christian charity on a scale to which we had never risen before. It was necessary so to act in order to give a reasonable chance of sixty millions of people being saved from their own vindictiveness. This had to be proven by some sincere act on the part of Britain, to clear her from the German persuasion that we were always talking about morals and never acting them, that while we talk of disinterestedness between nations and unselfishness and so on we build up our power over the world with marvellous success, hoodwinking one people and another with the loftiness of our pretensions'. [18] He later discussed a proposal made, and then rejected, by 'men of weight' of internationalising Gibraltar. He commented on this:

> If we intend to hold fast to everything we have gained in the past - and some of them possessions which have been gained by very questionable means - and we say that we are not going to part with a single inch of territory or a single privilege, all I can say is we are abandoning the principle of Christianity and taking once more our stand on the principle of competition. [19]

For Lyttelton to think such a sermon could pass without comment, or at least receive balanced discussion in wartime seems naive in the extreme. He admitted as much when apologising to one of the school's Governing Body:

If I had realised how my words to a quiet congregation were likely to be brought before the public, in imperfect form and with suggestive headlines, I should certainly have expressed myself differently... [20]

Certainly, Lyttelton received a rough ride in the papers. 'Headmaster of Eton's amazing address' was the headline to the summary given above. In the following days, editorials and letters pages - in the *Daily Mail, Daily Telegraph, Morning Post* and *Times* were mostly against him, sometimes vindictively so:

The 'Don't Humiliate Germany' speech of Dr Lyttelton, headmaster of Eton, has aroused protests in every class and in every part of the Country. From the flood of correspondence which reached the *Mail* during the weekend we print representative letters of indignation. All the letters expressed but one view; not a single one supported Dr Lyttelton. But we received one anonymous telegram from Croydon, saying, 'three cheers for Lyttelton'.

SIR; As an Old Etonian who is trying to do his bit, and father of an Etonian serving at the Front, may I add my humble endorsement of Sir Henry Craik's disgust and amazement at Dr Lyttelton's mischievous and most unseemly speech?

TO THE EDITOR OF THE MORNING POST: Since Dr Lyttelton's pro-German utterances many people have written to the papers urging patriotic parents to remove their boys from Eton. That would be a great mistake; the present Headmaster has no influence whatsoever on the feelings and opinions of Eton boys. The healthy virile tone which prevails at Eton is formed by the boys themselves, and the Head may have Socialists to preach to the boys, and he may try to teach them to love Germans, but he will never succeed in making Eton boys Socialists, or pro-Germans, or vegetarians or imbuing them with any silly fads.'

'Dr Lyttelton's Sermon circulated by Germany'. GERMANY is circulating throughout the neutral countries a sermon alleged to have been preached by the Rev. the Hon. Edward Lyttelton at St Margaret's Westminster. A diplomat remarked to me that the Wolff Bureau could not have done the thing better, adding that from what he knows of Dr Lyttelton he fears he is quite capable of making such a statement as is attributed to him. [21]

The Press were, then, unsparing, especially perhaps *The Times*, which maliciously carried a report at the foot of its letters page about the outbreak of 'German measles' at Eton, closing the school a day early for the holidays. In February 1916 it reported the arrest of Lyttelton's German housemaid for passing an uncensored letter to relatives in neutral Holland in a manner which put the Headmaster's household in a lurid light.

Lyttelton's career at Eton was clearly under threat, and some members of the Governing Body - who would decide his fate - were distinctly unsympathetic, especially when they contemplated the propaganda value of the remarks to the Germans. Lord Rosebery wrote in May 1915:

I am told that the Headmaster's allusion to Gibraltar has, not unnaturally, roused all Spain and revived that blister...I do not think that a resignation at Christmas would be at all premature or unwelcome. [22]

The Press reaction is perhaps understandable in the context of their daily stories of German atrocities. So far as Eton was concerned, 1,700 Old Boys were by now fighting, and Lyttelton was giving scores of memorial addresses for Etonians recently killed . Three senior boys at the school wrote to the *Times* in support of their headmaster:

We have heard many of his lectures and sermons...and most confidently assert that on no single occasion has he betrayed any tendency to that pro-Germanism of which he is being now so vehemently accused. [23]

Attitudes to war were being tested during the Lyttelton business. The editorials in the school *Chronicle* showed over time a marked shift, from 'Remember Louvain!' in 1914 to 'We are fighting for Freedom' in 1915, and in 1917 'Optimism about the War' – that is to say when might it end? Was the school doing very much to train its boys for fighting? The Officers' Training Corps, denuded of its Army Regular Adjutant for the duration of the war and officered by middle-aged masters, clearly had an important role to play. The prospect of active service was after all a reality for most boys, and one by no means distant. Sir Alexander Stanier, who was to join the Welsh Guards in 1917, recalls being offered a commission by a perhaps absent-minded Adjutant in London in 1915, when he was barely sixteen. Stanier replied that he might like to finish his schooldays first.

The *Chronicle* reported on the activities of the OTC on camp in 1915, where 'scientific' use of the bayonet was taught:

> Rapid progress was made in frightfulness, culminating in the awe-inspiring spectacle of six Eton officers, young in all but years, dashing irresistibly through the sacks, a torrent of sound and fury.' [24]

Quite what the OTC should be teaching was a matter for discussion. Some thought time should usefully be spent in it on 'machine-gunning and bombing'. But in general its efforts were perhaps not taken too seriously as being a world removed from the training to follow at Sandhurst and later at army depots such as the one in Sheppey - themselves at least early in the war a world removed from conditions in the trenches. What would seem to have been taken very seriously indeed was a sense of mission. As the prospect of conscription loomed, late in 1915, it was commented that:

> the opposition felt by a large proportion of the lower classes to compulsory service must be overcome. England is a Democracy...her people must therefore be led and not driven, and the lead must be taken by the Upper Classes. [25]

The *Chronicle's* attitude to the war changed as the years dragged on. The fourth year of fighting brought with it rationing. Conditions at Eton so far as food was concerned were worsening appreciably in 1917 and 1918, as this came into effect. Luxmoore commented to a friend, 'How are House Masters to manage? Schools are crowded because it's cheaper to send your boy there than to keep him at home.' [26]

Sir Steven Runciman, who arrived at Eton in 1916, commented that 'the food was so grim that I became more or less what would now be called anorexic.' [27] Lord Home, arriving in 1917, remembers being fed 'awful things' - among them 'Miss Marten's pudding' - a mixture of cold bacon fat, cold sausage and suet - 'simply revolting- one could hardly force it down.' [28]

A remedy for this shortage in supplies would seem to have presented itself. A newspaper feature in March 1917 showed sturdy 'Back to the Land' types - the Hon. Charles Rhys, Lord Dynevor's son, and J H O Tennant, hard at work digging potatoes on the playing fields. [29] The story bore the inevitable caption' The Playing Fields of Eton -1917.' Could this cutting and manuring of the sacred turf take the place of games? Perhaps, if properly organised, it could present an alternative. Luxmoore commented:

> The boys dig to some extent. Each house has an allotment and if it's not dug they mayn't enter for school events ! Each House has also to send a company to some farm for harvest work... [30]

But Parker quite properly points out that games remained the priority for the fields, not potatoes. One and a half acres only were ploughed, producing one and a half tons of potatoes in 1917. But more than forty acres remained for pitches.

Food shortages were apparently variable, with boys able to ensure supplies of fresh food from home winning popularity in their Boarding Houses. [31]

The end of the war, when it came, brought varied reactions. Some were crazy with joy; Lord Home remembers seeing a boy climbing on to a taxi and riding off on its roof in the direction of London. Luxmoore described the celebration of the Armistice to the son of a colleague serving in France:

> I feel more inclined to cry than to shout, thinking of all it has cost us. The boys are different, they paraded the town wrapped in flags and beating tom-toms and making those odious noises wh. nowadays are taken to express joy. [32]

But the recollection of Sir Steven Runciman is again different: 'I have to confess that I remember no particular ceremony on Armistice Day and certainly nothing in the nature of a Mafeking night: my only strong memory is one of seeing my brother in tears because he was going to miss the experience of joining so many of his contemporaries at the Front - he was just 18 at the time. I, being less romantic and very fond of him, was on the other hand delighted.' [33]

The War was over - with the loss of 1,157 Etonians. Eight of the names of the dead came the week

Sir Edgar Bertram McKennal,
Here I Am, 1923,
bronze figure, 74½" high.
Reproduced by courtesy of
Christie's.

Since I wrote to you I have received the papers with regard to an Eton memorial which is to cost the college £10,000 and Old Etonians £90,000. I suppose the College knows best whether it can afford £10,000 as a memorial. But as to the balance, have my colleagues any binding facts as to where this is to come? Remember the Old Etonian class is no longer a wealthy class. The only wealthy classes are the shipping and munitions people who are rarely, I suppose, Old Etonian. The Old Etonians are chiefly landlords. In this district landlords paying supertax will have to pay in local and Imperial burdens 11/6d. in the £... after the Peace, though this is not in sight, these burdens are not likely to cease... [35]

Thus restrained, the war memorials Eton acquired were a long set of bronze panels, prefixed with an inscription by M R James, with the names of the dead cast on them, along one wall of School Yard and a memorial window in College chapel. A series of tapestries in 'Henry VII Gothic' apparently depicting the life of St George were placed in Lower Chapel, [36] with the figures modelled by contemporary Etonians, the whole designed by a Mrs Akers-Douglas and woven at the William Morris looms.

More controversially, the school received a statue by Sir Bertram Mackennal, intended to be placed in the playing fields, of a naked youth, arms outstretched, 'stepping forward eagerly, but with due modesty, as one of many' [37] with the words of Samuel answering Eli's instructions in response to the voice of God in the Temple, 'Here I am, take me'. The statue was perhaps not universally well received. Luxmoore commented:

> ...of the statue I have heard no more; it stands, a grim spectacle in the dark passage of the Provost's Lodge swathed in white graveclothes from head to foot - covering all but the two black hands. I wonder any servant can be got to stay. [38]

The statue later was displayed in a more discreet setting than the Playing Fields, was disposed of in the 1960s and recently resurfaced at a Christie's auction. [39]

Apart from the memorials, there were great occasions to mark the ending of the war. On 20 May 1919 thirty-one Old Etonian generals were invited to a parade at the school; in the event eighteen came, among them Rawlinson, Plumer and Byng. They assembled in School Yard, on the steps of the chapel, and posed for a

after the Armistice. Various schemes to commemorate the dead had been proposed, as early as 1916, at which time Luxmoore had commented that 'Memorial schemes jostle like a Cubist picture'. [34]

Not that anything like a Cubist picture was actually envisaged. In common with almost all schools and for that matter most 'official' art, the memorials for those who had 'made a new world' were to be resolutely backward-looking. Eton had difficulties in that it had only recently completed - at very considerable expense - a vast and not especially beautiful Memorial Hall to the dead of the South African war. Luxmoore wanted anything to come in 1918-19 'to transcend and dominate' the memorial of the comparatively insignificant Boer War. A tower was proposed, or a cloister. But at this point concern seems to have been voiced as to how the vast cost of the war had affected, indirectly, even so wealthy a foundation as Eton. As early as November 1916, M R James had received the following reservations from Lord Rosebery:

Etonian generals revisit the College, May 1919.
Reproduced by permission of the Provost and Fellows of Eton College.

remarkable photograph with the Provost and Head Master. [40]

There is a marked irony about this photograph of the Etonian generals at Eton, for, by sitting on the steps to Chapel in School Yard, they were taking the place usually occupied for group photographs by the Collegers or the Eton Society. Only four years earlier, the eighteen members of this body, the self-elected oligarchy known as 'Pop', had been photographed on this very spot. Seven of those boys had been killed since then; several more badly wounded. The editor of the Eton College *Chronicle* in 1914, Henry Dundas, who had written the editorial 'Remember Louvain' had died in machine-gun fire at the Canal du Nord in September 1918. He was twenty-one. Sitting near him in the 'Pop', picture is Christopher Lighton, who served in the King's Royal Rifle Corps and was wounded

on the Somme. Nonetheless he survived to a great age and when interviewed about his experiences in July 1992 commented of the Somme:

> Even then we wondered just who was running this show- and what kind of brains they had. [41]

In May 1919, in School Yard, one is tempted to think he might have found his answer.

In producing both subalterns like Dundas and Lighton, and also the organisers both of the disasters of 1916 and the victories of 1918, not to mention a figure such as Edward Lyttelton, Eton's contribution to the First World War remains an ambiguous one. Perhaps it is best not to pass judgement, but merely to repeat the words on the memorials - Etona Non Immemor.

R.G. de Quetteville. (R.H. de M.)   V. Howard Vincent. (E.W.S)   V. A. Cazalet (R.P.L.B)   H. W. Houldsworth (P.W. F.E.R)

wounded. July 1st 1916. (M.C.) Yorkshire Reg.t P/W. March 1918 — D.S.O.   wounded Jan. 1916. 60th Rifles died South of France 1920.   1st Life Guards.   wounded May 1915 and May 1917 Seaforth Highlanders.

T. Philipson. (R.P.L.B)   R.H. Pike Pease. (A.A.S)   A.W. Greenfield. (A.A.R.)   W.G. Edmonstone. (P.V.B)

2nd Life Guards.   killed Sept. 15. 1916. Coldstream Guards.   killed October. 1916 Rifle Brigade.   killed Sept. 15. 1916. Coldstream Guards.

**Leaving portraits from C H Lighton's album.
Reproduced by permission of the Provost and Fellows of Eton College.**

Notes

1. Of 5,660 Etonians who served in the First World War, some 1,157 were killed: 20.5% of the total. The losses sustained by some other schools were even higher: 23% in the case of Downside and Fettes, 27% in that of Harrow.

2. In the school *Chronicle* for 28 October 1914 the forthcoming 'Wall Game' played on St Andrew's Day had been discussed in the following terms: 'Well, you want to know about Saturday, do you? At precisely 12.25 we shall goose-step down to the ground singing, "College uber alles". At 12.30 we shall commence the attack with heavy howitzers, shortly followed by the assault, in close formation; then we shall destroy the Wall, school buildings, Memorial hall

and the civilian population. No quarter will be given to journalists'.
3. Peter Parker, *The Old Lie: The Great War and the Public School Ethos*, London, Constable and Co, 1987.
4. Casualty lists show a preponderance of young Etonians in regiments such as the Seaforth Highlanders or the Welch Fusiliers, and from the household division; but it has been observed that this phenomenon was perhaps more marked in the Second World War. In the First, it was quite frequent for a young Etonian to join his county regiment, often those recently raised; the Guards officers tended to be those who may well have been destined for a military career in any event. Marcus Wright (b.1896) left in September 1914 and joined the Loyal North Lancs Regiment, as befitted his

family's spinning interests there. The Provost's son reportedly came to the school quite frequently to recruit for officers for the Rifle Brigade. In overall numbers, 727 were in cavalry regiments, 410 in the Royal Artillery, and 2,648 were in infantry regiments (818 Foot Guards). These later figures, however, include regular officers serving in 1914.
5. H E Luxmoore to C W Christie, December 1914.
6. Eton College *Chronicle*, 27 May 1915.
7. H E Luxmoore to Christopher Stone, 11 October 1918. E Coll MS Luxmoore/58. The practice of special evening services in Chapel in time of war was followed at Eton during the Gulf War.
8. Eton College *Chronicle*, 14 October 1915.

9. Hugh MacNaghten in the Eton College *Chronicle*, 28 October 1915.
10. See illustration.
11. FIetcher had been Captain of the School in 1905 and his death certainly seemed to make a great impression. He had returned to teach at Eton only in 1913, and his father took his place as he went to put his French to use as a liaison officer with the French forces. It was at the Bois Grenier that he daringly crossed German lines to retrieve a captured French flag with which the enemy had been taunting the French. He was killed two days after this feat. The flag, left by his parents, hangs in College chapel. Thirteen Etonians were to receive the Victoria Cross, and one, George Schack-Somer, a mining engineer working in Russia at the outbreak of war, the equivalent

csarist order of St Anne. Schack-Somer, a corporal in the 12th Artirsky Hussars, was idolised by the British press for his decoration, awarded for the capture of an Austrian trench. He was however fatally wounded in June 1915. Among the recipients of the Victoria Cross was one of the fire-eating Borton brothers, who between them were mentioned in dispatches nine times and both received the DSO. Lt-Col Borton, serving in the KRRC in Palestine, encouraged his men to capture a Turkish trench by the feat of dribbling a football towards it across No Man's Land.

12. Eton College *Chronicle*, 7 October 1915.

13. Son of Eton House Master.

14. Eton College *Chronicle*, 22 July 1915.

15. Eton College Chronicle, 15 October 1914. 'The Head Master made a most impressive speech in which, after pointing out the absurdity of modern war in which half our energies are directed towards killing as many people as possible, and the other half towards keeping them alive, he declared that there could be no hope of lasting peace unless the nations adopted a new attitude and abandoned all selfish patriotism.' (Later in the debate the President of the society 'feared we might sink into a state of selfish and luxurious indolence if the country never experienced the stimulating effect of the fear of war.')

16. H E Luxmoore to Mrs Coode, May 1915.

17. It was not the first controversy in which Lyttelton, whose brother had been a Cabinet minister, had been involved. In 1908, shortly after his arrival as Head Master, he had permitted a delegation of unemployed men en route to petition the King at Windsor to address the boys in School Yard, or as one critic put it 'to desecrate the Headmaster's steps'. He is certainly remembered as an eccentric, with a mania for fresh air extending to sleeping with his head out of doors or teaching boys' divisions outside in School Yard with hoar frost on the ground. After his resignation he went to work with Canon Dick Sheppard as curate of St Martin-in-the-Fields.

18. Though the similarity is coincidental, it can be said that at least one Old Etonian, and one 'doing his bit', the observer pilot Thomas Hughes was by 1918 able to confide to his diary ideas not dissimilar to Lyttelton's. He wrote on New Year's Day 1918, 'Let us look back on the achievements of the past three and a half years which have justified the slight sacrifice we have all so gladly made. What are these achievements? We have -er- held our own against the-er- numerically and morally inferior hordes of our assailants. We have -er- shown the whole world that Britain is fighting as she has always fought- in India, Ireland, S. Africa and elsewhere - to uphold the rights of the smaller nationalities to determine their own destinies and forms of government, and to redress the wrongs of the weak. We have from time to time set before ourselves many noble aims, modified from time to time by our inability to carry them out or by our realisation of their unprofitable nature.' Source given in Malcolm Brown, *The Imperial War Museum Book of The First World War*, Sidgwick and Jackson, London, 1991, p 273. Hughes left Eton in 1902, enlisted as a private soldier in 1914 and joined the RFC in 1916. He was killed in an accident in September 1918.

19. Summary of the sermon given in The *Times*, 27 March 1915.

20. E Lyttelton to M R James, 27 April 1915. Coll MS 396.

21. *Morning Post*, 30 March 1915.

22. Lord Rosebery to M R James, 12 May 1915. E Coll MS 396. In fact Lyttelton was at length induced to resign with effect from December 1916.

23. *Times*, 30 March 1915. The three boys concerned were Caroe, Cazalet (Victor Cazalet, later an MP; Life Guards; served in France and Siberia; awarded MC; his elder brother was killed at Ginchy in 1916) and Cust (Artillery in 1916, and taken prisoner).

24. Eton College *Chronicle*, 30 September 1915.

25. Eton College *Chronicle*, 14 October 1915.

26. H E Luxmoore to C A Kirby, 1 March 1918.

27. Letter to the author, August 1992.

28. In a recorded interview with the author, July 1992.

29. *Daily Graphic*, 5 March 1917.

30. H E Luxmoore to G H Tristram, 15 May 1916.

31. Brigadier P B E Acland (d.1993), the present Provost's father, was at Eton from 1915 and recalled of the food in his schooldays that his house master (E L 'Jelly' Churchill) 'saw us all right'.

32. H E Luxmoore to Christopher Stone, 11 November 1918.

33. Letter to the author, August 1992.

34. H E Luxmoore to Lord Gerald Wellesley, 29 November 1918.

35. Lord Rosebery to M R James, 18 November 1916. E Coll MS P6/8/55. M R James was Provost of King's College, Cambridge at the time of this letter, and an ex-officio Fellow of Eton; he was acting on behalf of Edmund Warre, the Provost of Eton, too ill to deal with business. James succeeded him as Provost of Eton in 1918.

36. A building of great ugliness added in 1891 when the numbers at Eton had swollen so much that it was impossible to accommodate the whole school in one building for worship.

37. Charles Marriot in *Country Life*, 23 July 1923.

38. H E Luxmoore to Lord Gerald Wellesley, 3 December 1923. But Luxmoore had himself in 1917 commissioned a memorial to the fallen Logie Leggatt, to be awarded to the succeeding Captains of the College 'Wall Game' team; it, too, depicted a naked youth.

39. I am indebted to Dr T P Connor for information concerning the War Memorials at Eton.

40. C A Alington had replaced Lyttelton in December 1916.

41. Lt-Col Sir Christopher Lighton Bt, in a recorded interview with the author, July 1992.

Further Reading

The forthcoming *History of Eton College* by T S B Card will contain a chapter on Eton's experience of the war. The service records of Etonians who fought are to be found in *Etonians who fought in the Great War MCMXIV-MCMXVIII*, Medici Society, 1921. Biographies of Etonian figures serving in the Great War abound; but Nicholas Mosley's biography of Julian Grenfell (Weidenfeld and Nicholson, 1976) and Wilfrid Blunt's *John Christie of Glyndebourne* (Geoffrey Bles, 1968) would seem among the best. The story of the Borton brothers can be found in *My Warrior Sons* by A C Borton (ed. Guy Slater, Peter Davies, 1973). There is an account of Lyttelton's sermon in Alan Wilkinson's *The Church of England and the First World War* (SPCK, 1981). For a wider survey of public schools and the Great War, *The Old Lie: The Great War and the Public School Ethos* by Peter Parker (Constable, 1987) displays its colours pretty plainly but provides a wealth of information and a much fuller bibliography than is possible here.

The German battlecruiser attack on the east coast ports, 16 December 1914

John Bullen

John Bullen is a research assistant in the Department of Exhibits and Firearms.

To penetrate the little port at nine o'clock was to walk through a silent city of the dead. One could scarcely realise at first that this was England as one walked through silent streets, the tramp of one's boots upon the pavement seemingly intensified. In the black darkness not a light was to be seen, under martial law all had been forced indoors. [1]

At the outbreak of war on 4 August 1914, the greatest concentration of naval power in the world was deployed around the North Sea. The Royal Navy had twenty nine capital ships - twenty dreadnoughts and nine battlecruisers - with twelve battleships and one battlecruiser building. Three further dreadnoughts which were being constructed, two for Ottoman Turkey and one for Chile, were quickly requisitioned. The Royal Navy also possessed forty one pre-dreadnoughts. The High Seas Fleet had thirteen battleships and five battlecruisers, with seven battleships and three battlecruisers being constructed. The Imperial German Navy also possessed twenty three pre-dreadnoughts. [2]

Under orders from Kaiser Wilhelm, the Supreme War Lord, and Supreme Headquarters, Admiral Hugo von Pohl, Chief of the Admiralty Staff (*Admiralstab*) concentrated the High Seas Fleet in its Jade anchorage and adopted a 'fleet in being' strategy.

The German Admiralty Staff gauged that the Royal Navy's anticipated close blockade of Germany would provide opportunities for submarines, torpedo boats and minelayers to erode the Grand Fleet's capital ship strength: the High Seas Fleet would sortie and, in a naval *guerre à outrance*, challenge the Grand Fleet for the 'command of the seas'.

The reversal of the Royal Navy's blockading tactics negated Germany's strategy. Yet events at sea over the next months led ultimately to heavy units of the *Hochseeflotte* attacking east coast ports. The German losses of three cruisers and a destroyer at the battle of the Heligoland Bight on 28 August 1914 were balanced by the loss of the British cruisers *Aboukir*, *Hogue*, and *Cressy* on 22 September to the submarine U-9. At the end of October came the German Navy's greatest victories. On 27 October, the brand new dreadnought HMS *Audacious* was mined and sunk off the coast of northern Ireland, and on 1 November Vice-Admiral Maximilian Graf von Spee's crack Pacific cruiser squadron met and overwhelmed Rear-Admiral Sir Christopher Craddock's weak South American squadron in the Battle of Coronel. [3] The High Seas Fleet was jubilant. The Admiralty under Fisher, First Sea Lord, and Winston Churchill, First Lord, swiftly replied. The battle cruisers *Invincible* and *Inflexible* under Vice-Admiral Sir Doveton Sturdee were detached from the Grand Fleet to destroy von Spee's squadron.

On 3 November, Rear-Admiral Franz von Hipper's First Scouting Group comprising the battlecruisers *Seydlitz, Moltke, Von der Tann*, and the armoured cruiser *Blucher*, bombarded Yarmouth on the Norfolk coast. It was a diversionary attack to cover a mining operation. This new aggressive policy stemmed from pressure from both Grand Admiral Alfred von Tirpitz, State Secretary of the Navy and Admiral Friederich von Ingenohl, Commander-in-Chief of the High Seas Fleet, to maintain the momentum of the recent German successes at sea. [4]

Admiral Fisher, in turn, was convinced that the Germans, taking advantage of the numerically reduced Grand Fleet, would plan a further major raid on the east coast. Admiral Sir John Jellicoe, C-in-C of the Grand Fleet, pinpointed 8 December as the likely date, since there would be no moon and the high tides would be propitious for a German night sortie by heavy units.

This, indeed, was the case. In mid-November, von Ingenohl had determined on a raid against the east coast ports of Hartlepool and Scarborough, which was approved by Kaiser Wilhelm, who had been overjoyed by the Coronel victory. The *Admiralstab* decreed, however, that the First Scouting Group must be at full strength for the operation. This meant that the attack had to be delayed until mid-December to allow machinery defects in the *Von der Tann* to be remedied. [5]

The raid had several purposes: to tie down disproportionate numbers of the Royal Navy's warships; to inflict damage on British ports and their industrial resources; to bring home to the British people Germany's war-making capabilities; to convince the German people of the value of the expensive High Seas Fleet; to maintain morale in the *Hochseeflotte* by successful raiding; and to lure and, if possible, cut off and destroy a squadron of British capital ships, and thereby reduce the Grand Fleet's numerical superiority.

On 8 December Sturdee's battlecruiser squadron and escorts virtually wiped out von Spee's Pacific squadron in the Battle of the Falklands. Von Ingenohl resolved on a bold and morale-boosting counterstroke. The operation by the First Scouting Group against Hartlepool and Scarborough would go ahead while the light cruiser SMS *Kolberg* of the Second Scouting Group would lay mines off Filey.

The Germans had been stung by von Spee's annihilation, yet were ignorant, and remained ignorant throughout the First World War, of a far greater British victory. By December 1914, the British possessed the keys to the three main German maritime and diplomatic radio communications codes. The HVB code - *Handelsverkehrbuch* - used by U-boats, small warships, Zeppelin airships, and merchant ships had been discovered on 11 August 1914 when the Royal Australian Navy captured the German steamer *Hobart* in Port Phillip Bay, near Melbourne. On 26 August the light cruiser SMS *Magdeburg* ran aground on Odensholm Island at the entrance to the Gulf of Finland. The Russians, who boarded her, found three copies of the SKM - *Signalbuch der Kaiserlichen Marine* - the major unit code, and generously gave the best preserved volume to the British. This precious gift arrived at the Admiralty on 13 October. The third code, VB - *Verkehrsbuch* - was obtained by chance. A British fishing vessel was working the Broad Fourteens, an area off the Dutch Coast, and brought up a chest containing cipher material which had been dumped by the German torpedo boat S-119, sunk in an encounter on 17 October. The VB code was employed between Berlin and its embassies and consulates, and by detached warships in foreign waters. The British set up their cryptography centre in Room 40 of the Old Admiralty Building, off Whitehall, to absorb and decipher this massive signals traffic. It was an astonishing coup. [6]

The Imperial German Navy, emboldened by the knowledge of the absence of two British battlecruisers in the southern oceans, and the loss of the *Audacious*, moved swiftly. The U-27 reconnoitred the target areas off the east coast and confirmed that coastal defences were weak and British minefields non-existent.

Von Ingenohl's plan was for Hipper to sail early on 15 December, while he would follow with the main force of the High Seas Fleet in the evening. The bombardment of the English towns would begin at first light on 16 December. Hipper had signalled a request on 14 December for extensive reconnaissance flights by airships and aircraft to the west, north-west and north on 15 and 16 December. Hipper added that German forces would be at sea, leaving the Jade at 0330 and passing Heligoland at 0530 on 15 December.

Room 40 absorbed this information from the heavy wireless traffic, some of which was transmitted in the vital HVB code. Just before midnight on 14 December, Admiral Jellicoe received the following signal from the Admiralty:

Good information has just been received showing that a German cruiser squadron with destroyers will leave the Jade on Tuesday morning early (15 December) and return on Wednesday night. It is apparent from our information that the battleships are very unlikely to come out. The enemy will have time to reach our coast. Send at once, leaving tonight, the battlecruiser Squadron and Light Cruiser Squadron supported by a Battle Squadron, preferably the Second. At dawn on Wednesday (16 December) they should be at some point where they can intercept the enemy on his return. Tyrwhitt with his light cruisers and destroyers (the Harwich Force) will try to get in touch with the enemy off the British coast and shadow him, keeping the Admiral informed. From our information the German cruiser squadron consists of four battle cruisers and five light cruisers and there will probably be three flotillas of destroyers.[7]

Room 40's cryptographers had accurately forecast the movements of Hipper's squadrons, but had not confirmed that the entire High Seas Fleet would provide distant cover. The Admiralty, therefore, ordered south only a detachment of the Grand Fleet's strength, principally Vice-Admiral Sir David Beatty's First Battle-Cruiser Squadron comprising *Lion* (flag), *New Zealand, Tiger*, and *Queen Mary* based at Cromarty: and Vice-Admiral Sir George S Warrender's Second Battle Squadron comprising the most powerful homogeneous squadron of the Grand Fleet at the time, the 13.5 inch gunned *King George V* (flag), *Orion, Ajax, Centurion, Monarch* and *Conqueror*, based at Scapa. Supporting cruiser, destroyer and submarine squadrons were also ordered to sea. Beatty and Warrender were to rendezvous at first light on 16 December off the south-east corner of the Dogger Bank. This position, selected by Jellicoe, was on an almost direct line from Scarborough, a German objective, to Heligoland; 180 miles from the former and a 110 miles from the latter. [8]

The Admiralty gambled on a tactical trade-off in return for major strategic results: in effect, allowing Hipper to attack the east coast objectives before intervening decisively with Beatty's and Warrender's battle squadrons. The loss of all or most of Hipper's battlecruisers to the Royal Navy would be a prize outweighing any losses or damage inflicted by the German naval attack on the coastal ports.

At 0300 on 15 December Hipper's First

The German battlecruiser *Derfflinger*. This class, which included the *Lutzow*, were the best fighting capital ships of the First World War apart from the British 15-inch gunned *Queen Elizabeth* class. *Derfflinger* displaced 30,700 tons deep load, was 690ft 3in x 95ft 2in x 31ft deep load. She was armed with eight 30.5cms (12in) guns, twelve 15cm (5.9 inch) guns, four 8.8cm (3.45in) guns, and four 50cm (19.7in) torpedo tubes. She had a main armoured belt of 12 inches, a maximum speed of 26.5 knots and a complement of 1,112 men. SP2691

Scouting Group comprising the battlecruisers *Seydlitz, Derfflinger, Moltke, Von der Tann* and the large armoured cruiser *Blucher*, with the escorting light cruisers of the Second Scouting Group and its two flotillas of torpedo boats, sailed from the Jade. Admiral von Ingenohl's battle squadrons left Cuxhaven during the afternoon and the whole force rendezvoused north of Heligoland. After dark, Hipper's force sailed on its bombardment mission, followed by von Ingenohl's force which comprised nearly all the *Hochseeflotte's* modern capital ships. Von Ingenohl had deployed his fourteen dreadnoughts and eight pre-dreadnoughts into three battle squadrons in line ahead: to starboard were positioned five light cruisers; to port was the light cruiser *Rostock* and the Fifth and Seventh Flotillas (torpedo boats); astern were the Second and Eighth Flotillas; and ahead of the main battle squadrons were the armoured cruisers *Roon* and *Prinz Heinrich*, the light cruiser *Hamburg* and the Sixth Flotilla. [9]

Meanwhile, the battle squadrons of Warrender, who was in command, and Beatty had met off the Moray Firth, and by midnight of 15/16 December were approaching the Dogger Bank. At approximately 0515, 16 December, just south of the Dogger Bank, and before first light, Warrender's destroyers encountered the German destroyer V-155, part of the advanced screen's Sixth Flotilla. A confused, if hard-fought, action between British destroyers and German destroyers and cruisers now followed. V-155's first wireless reports on the two-hour encounter came in at approximately 0530. At this time less than ten miles separated the *Prinz Heinrich* from Warrender's 2nd Battle Squadron. [10]

As a result of the Admiralty's instructions to

Jellicoe, a tactical situation had arisen which was not to occur again during the First World War, and which neither side, at the time, appreciated. The High Seas Fleet was presented with the opportunity of crushing two isolated but powerful squadrons of the Grand Fleet's capital ships and achieving, at one stroke, numerical parity with the Royal Navy in the North Sea. The Royal Navy, conversely, was to be offered the glittering prize of annihilating Hipper's elite First Scouting Group and establishing absolute supremacy in the North Sea.

On receipt of V-155's signal, von Ingenohl ordered a turn to port and, as the confused fighting continued, signalled a further turn to port at 0620 and withdrew with all his capital ships at high speed for Cuxhaven. Von Ingenohl's withdrawal was conditioned by several factors: he believed that the British destroyers were the advanced screen of the entire Grand Fleet; he expected a massed torpedo boat attack on the High Seas Fleet; and he was ever mindful of *Admiralstab* instructions: [11]

> The fleet must therefore be held back and avoid action which might lead to heavy losses. This does not, however, prevent favourable opportunities being used to damage the enemy. Employment of the fleet outside the [Heligoland] Bight which the enemy tries to bring about by his movements in the Skagerrack is not mentioned in the orders for operations as being one of such favourable operations. [12]

Von Ingenohl believed that he had transgressed these instructions. His withdrawal left Hipper's battlecruisers isolated and vulnerable to Warrender's two battle squadrons. Warrender, as yet, was not aware of Hipper's position.

The weather steadily worsened. At 0632 Hipper, unsure of his exact position, ordered his escorts, apart from the minelaying cruiser *Kolberg*, to return and rendezvous with the *Hochseeflotte*. At 0640 Hipper fixed his position off the English coast and divided the First Scouting Group. *Derfflinger*, *Von der Tann* and *Kolberg*, under Rear Admiral Tapken, headed south for Scarborough and Whitby, while Hipper took *Seydlitz*, *Moltke* and *Blucher* north-west to bombard Hartlepool. [13]

Of the three English coastal ports only the ship-building town of Hartlepool, which was a defended port and a flotilla base to the light cruisers *Patrol* and *Forward*, four River-class destroyers, and the assigned submarine C-9, could be classed as a legitimate target according to the Hague Convention, one of whose

articles stated: 'The bombardment by naval forces of undefended ports, towns, villages, dwellings, or buildings is forbidden'. [14] The last time Hartlepool had experienced a major attack from the sea was by Danish Vikings in 800 AD, who destroyed a monastery founded in 640 AD.

Scarborough and Whitby had more dramatic histories. Scarborough had been attacked from the sea in 1066 when Harald Hardrada, the last great Viking hero, and Harald Godwinson's half-brother Tostig, had landed from their long ships and sacked the town. Naval guns were heard in September 1779 when Paul Jones, in command of a Franco-American squadron, captured two British warships in sight of Scarborough after a fierce engagement. Whitby's history, especially in association with its splendid Abbey, was long and eventful. Its last experience of naval warfare had been in June 1636 when two Dutch warships, in defiance of English neutrality, had chased a Spanish ship into Whitby harbour and boarded her. The Governor of Whitby, Sir Hugh Cholmly, had reacted spiritedly, and, taking ships, had recaptured the Spanish ship and seized the Dutch captains. [15] In December 1914, Scarborough was a fishing port, but was renowned as the leading holiday resort on the east coast, possessing many fine hotels. Whitby, too, was a fishing port, and also possessed substantial hotels and holidaying facilities.

The ordeal of the east coast ports began at 0755 hours on Wednesday 16 December, when the grey shapes of Tapken's *Derfflinger*, *Von der Tann* and *Kolberg* appeared out of the fog off Scarborough and opened a heavy fire on the Falsgrave suburb, which contained a radio station. The warships then turned north off the White Nab to bombard the town. *Derfflinger* and *Von der Tann* closed to between 2,000 and 3,000 yards and opened a heavy fire. A resident of Scarborough later recalled:

> There was a noise like thunder, plaster at once began to fall from the ceiling, and going to the door I saw crowds of people running along the street ... Houses were falling to pieces as we ran up Albemarle Road and crowds of people were making for the station. [16]

For half an hour approximately 500 shells ranging in calibre from 12-inch, 11-inch to 5.9-inch were poured into the town. Damage to property was severe. A turret of the Royal Hotel was blown away, and part of the seaward front of the imposing Grand Hotel destroyed. Several churches and a hospital in Auborough Street, were damaged. Yet casualties were remarkably light in relation

John Shield Ryalls, fourteen month old victim of the bombardment in the arms of Miss Bertha McIntyre, who was also killed. Q53464

May and Test, under Lieutenant Commander H M Fraser in Doon, sighted the German warships to the south-east at a range of 9,000 yards. Seydlitz, Moltke and Blucher opened fire with their main and secondary armaments and, amidst a hail of 11-inch, 8.2-inch, and 5.9-inch fire, the destroyers turned away to the north except for the Doon which attempted to launch a torpedo. The range, now down to 5,000 yards, was still too great for the Doon's torpedo and the destroyer withdrew with eleven casualties and riddled with shell splinters. [19]

At 0803 the German warships opened a general bombardment of Hartlepool at a range of two miles. The initial target was the old Borough of Hartlepool, the small town which contained the docks and harbour and which was separated at this time from the larger West Hartlepool. One eyewitness, Mr W N Collins, then seventeen years of age, described the opening of the German shelling:

> A tremendous explosion rocked the house followed by an inferno of noise and the reek of high explosives, and as I made for the door clouds of brick dust and smoke eddied around. The seafront was only 50 yards away and I ran towards it. On my left a short distance away stood the Lighthouse and our home was near the shore end of the concrete breakwater which pointed for 500 yards almost due East ... and to the right was the entrance to the Docks and Harbour ... I was amazed to see three huge grey Battle-cruisers which looked only a few hundred yards from the end of the breakwater. Their massive guns were firing broadsides and in the dull light of a winter's morning it was like looking into a furnace. [20]

Hartlepool made a spirited reply to the powerful German warships looming out of the North Sea mist. It possessed two batteries of 6-inch guns, the two-gun Heugh Battery and the one gun of the Lighthouse Battery. The guns were 6-inch Mk7 coast defence guns of a model introduced in 1898. [21] The Hartlepool batteries were manned by men of the Durham Royal Garrison Artillery (Territorial Forces) under the command of Lieutenant-Colonel Robson, a former mayor of the town.

> The air was torn to shreds by explosives. I had never been under fire before and at first did not realise what was causing the high-pitched shrieks, then it dawned on me that it was the

to the number of shells fired. Seventeen were killed including a baby and two children, and several hundred people were treated for injuries.

There were numerous stories of narrow escapes and English sang-froid. During the shelling, Special Constable R Warriner and Coastguard Mason found that a shell had destroyed the flag staff at the coastguard station on Castle Hill. They secured the Union Flag to a telegraph pole. 'Are we downhearted?' demanded Warriner of Mason, amidst the explosions. 'No!' came the latter's defiant reply. [17]

Meanwhile, Hartlepool was suffering a bloodier martyrdom. Alerted by Room 40, the Admiralty had instructed all warships out on patrol. The deteriorating weather led Commodore First Class George Ballard, the Admiral of Patrols, to order his captains to remain in harbour with steam up unless required. The Senior Naval Officer at Hartlepool, Captain A C Bruce, sent out the four River-class destroyers but the two light cruisers Patrol and Forward and the submarine C-9 remained in harbour. [18]

At 0755 the four destroyers, Doon, Waveney,

whistle of hundreds of shells rushing over my head at low altitude. The great guns of the warships continued to belch flames continuously. [22]

The Royal Navy attempted to engage the German heavy units. HMS *Patrol* cast off from the jetty at 0818 as a hail of shot fell into the harbour. Workmen aboard a small steamer furiously cheered *Patrol's* gallant sortie until shell hits dispersed them and sank the steamer. As *Patrol* passed the entrances to the small harbour she was hit by two 11-inch and one 5.9-inch shell and was hastily grounded by Captain Bruce to make emergency repairs. [23] The submarine C-9, potentially the German battlecruisers' most dangerous adversary, had dived to avoid the shellfire and while under way had grounded at the bar to the harbour entrance. [24] The bombardment was over before C-9 had cleared the shoal. HMS *Forward* was not able to raise steam in time.

Through the fog, mist and gunsmoke the duel between the shore batteries and the battlecruisers continued. *Seydlitz* and *Moltke* initially concentrated their fire on the Heugh battery for fifteen minutes, while *Blucher* bombarded the port. Not a single 6-inch gun was put out of action, although casualties were inflicted. *Seydlitz* and *Moltke* then bombarded the town, while *Blucher* engaged the batteries at a range of 4,000 yards. [25]

The British gunners could not cripple or sink the tough German battlecruisers with their 100lb 6-inch shells, but damaging hits were registered. *Seydlitz* was hit three times, *Moltke* once and *Blucher* four times. One shell demolished part of *Blucher's* forebridge, another damaged one of her main six 8.2-inch gun turrets, and two more knocked out two of her sixteen 8.8 cm (3.45-ins) guns and inflicted casualties of nine killed and two wounded. [26]

Hartlepool, in turn, suffered severely. Mr Collins's experiences were typical:

> Buildings near me were in ruins and as I rounded the corner of Lumley Street I saw the body of Sammy Woods, a school-friend of mine, lying half out of the doorway, a shell having burst just as he stepped out a second before I turned the corner. [27]

Mr Collins made his way through the town and skirted by the dock area, passing an iron railway bridge under which people were sheltering.

> Shells dropping among the stacks of timber [for the Durham coalmines] blew them into the air like feathers. About the same time the gasometer received a direct hit and blew up, cutting off supplies to the town. The noise of the shells passing over or exploding was incessant, but now many were going over to West Hartlepool, the larger of the two towns. People were hurrying out of town and making for the open country towards the village of Hart a few miles north of Hartlepool, and they carried their most precious possessions. [28]

At 0852 the Germans fired their last shell at a range of 9,200 yards as they withdrew. *Seydlitz*, *Moltke* and *Blucher* had poured 1,150 rounds of heavy and medium calibre shells into the town. The total British casualties were 102 killed, including nine soldiers, seven sailors and fifteen children, and 467 wounded, of whom 43 were military personnel. Damage to military installations was minimal, but seven churches, ten public buildings, five hotels, and over 300 houses were damaged. [29]

The bombardment had been one-sided, but the British gunners had fought bravely and fired 123 rounds. The volume of effective fire had been reduced by the proximity of the lighthouse which blocked the line of fire south of the Heugh battery and to the north of the 6-inch gun position near the lighthouse itself. The heavy mist also impaired visibility and accurate fire, but this factor, on balance, favoured the British.

Von der Tann and *Derfflinger* had sailed north after bombarding Scarborough to join Hipper's squadron which was withdrawing from Hartlepool. The *Kolberg* had continued south and laid a hundred mines off Filey. Now came the Germans' last blow. At 0900 *Von der Tann* and *Derfflinger* opened fire on Whitby signal station and town and in ten minutes fired nearly 200 rounds of 5.9-inch and 3.45-inch shell fire. The casualties in Whitby of two men killed and three wounded were remarkably light, in spite of severe damage to the town and also some to the historic abbey. By 0930 Hipper's First Scouting Group and the *Kolberg* had joined up and, at 23 knots, were steaming hard for the Heligoland Bight. [30]

By 0730 Warrender and Beatty had reached the rendezvous south-east of the Dogger Bank. At 0805 Beatty received a delayed destroyer report that the large German cruiser *Roon* and five destroyers were being shadowed, a report which Warrender had received a quarter of an hour earlier. Beatty and the First Battle-Cruiser Squadron and escorts were already steering a similar course at 18 knots. *Roon* and her destroyers were, at this time, astern of the *Hochseeflotte* which Beatty and Warrender were unwittingly chasing.

Ruins of a home in Scarborough where five members of one family were killed during the bombardment. Q53463

Whitby Abbey - partially destroyed during the Dissolution of the Monasteries - looms over yet more devastation, wrought this time by the German bombardment. Q53459

From 0819 the Admiralty had intercepted signals from Fraser's destroyers off Hartlepool and by 0840 signals from both Scarborough and Hartlepool. The anticipated attack on the east coast by German heavy ships was taking place. A little after 0900 both Warrender and Beatty had turned west and were making for the English north-east coast, by 0935 steaming hard in two formations separated by ten miles to intercept Hipper's First Scouting Group. The latter was racing for home, ignorant both of the deadly presence of ten British capital ships and other escorts attempting to close with and destroy them, or that the *Hochseeflotte* was returning to harbour leaving Hipper's squadron isolated. [31]

At 1011 Jellicoe intuitively informed Warrender that Hipper would escape through a twenty-mile gap off Whitby through the German minefields recently laid off the Tyne and Humber. Hipper, indeed, followed this route. Jellicoe took the added precaution of ordering the 3rd Battle Squadron of eight 12-inch gunned pre-dreadnoughts south from Rosyth to block the Germans if they attempted to escape to the north inside the minefields. Churchill gave a graphic description of the events, as seen in the Admiralty War Room in Whitehall:

> Only one thing could enable the Germans to escape annihilation at the hands of an overwhelmingly superior force ... The word 'Visibility' assumed a sinister significance. Warrender and Beatty had horizons of nearly ten miles ... We went on tenterhooks to breakfast. To have this tremendous prize - the German battle-cruiser squadron whose loss would fatally mutilate the whole German Navy and could never be repaired - actually within our claws, and to have the event turn upon a veil of mist was a racking ordeal. [32]

At approximately 1100 hours the two forces were about a hundred miles apart and approaching each other at a combined speed of over forty knots. Then, as Churchill feared, the unpredictable North Sea weather turned foul and high seas and driving rain reduced visibility to a little over a mile. Nevertheless, at 1125 the cruiser *Southampton*, the most southerly ship of Beatty's scouting light cruiser forces, sighted a German light cruiser and destroyer force which was screening Hipper's First Scouting Group and engaged at 1130.

However, a badly phrased signal from Beatty's Flag Lieutenant, Ralph Seymour, ultimately caused the *Southampton* and a supporting light cruiser, the *Birmingham*, to break off the action. The aggressive Hipper, alerted by these movements, altered course from east to south-east at 1150 hours to support his light forces. But at 1215 Beatty was angered to learn that his cruisers had lost contact with the enemy. [33]

Hipper's luck held. At 1215 Warrender, now 15 miles south-east of Beatty, and the light German forces sighted each other. The German screen was forty miles ahead of the First Scouting Group. Hipper, forewarned of the strength of Warrender's force of six dreadnoughts, turned north of the Dogger Bank and steamed hard for Heligoland, shielded by rain squalls. Beatty received news of Warrender's sighting at 1225 and turned east to place himself between Hipper and the Jade. But Hipper had eluded both the First Battle Cruiser Squadron and the Second Battle Squadron. A last attempt to deploy submarines and destroyers to intercept the German forces also failed. [34]

The aftermath of the raid in both countries was predictable. There was jubilation in Germany, and the Kaiser was delighted. The *Berliner Tageblatt* proclaimed 'Once more our naval forces, braving the danger of scattered mines in the German Ocean [North Sea], have shelled English fortified places'; and the *Berliner Neuste Nachtichtenblatt* extolled this 'further proof of the gallantry of our Navy'. [35]

In Britain, inevitably, there was outrage. *The Times* stated that 'For the first time for many centuries the coast of England has been directly and seriously attacked', [36] and condemned the German politician Count Ernst von Reventlow who had written to a German newspaper that 'We must see clearly that in order to fight with success we must fight ruthlessly in the proper meaning of the word'. [37] German ruthlessness had provoked English anger. At the inquest for the dead of Scarborough, the foreman of the jury, Mr Plummer Yeoman, had urged a verdict of 'wilful murder', but on the advice of the Coroner, Mr George Taylor, a verdict of 'killed during the bombardment of the town by an enemy ship' [38] was returned.

The overall effect of the raids on the British people was to provoke a mixture of hatred of the Hun 'baby killers' and to kindle a renewed commitment to the war effort. At Hartlepool, which had borne the brunt of the bombardment, the bravery of the 6-inch guns' crews was acknowledged by the award of the DSO to Colonel Robson and one DCM and two MMs to other deserving gunners. The courage displayed by the Royal Navy was appreciated, too, in a moving testimonial sent by the townspeople of Hartlepool to Captain Bruce:

> The Committee representing the tradesmen of The Hartlepool and District Traders' Defence Association thereby express their admiration of the gallant conduct of the Officers and Men of His Majesty's Ships stationed at Hartlepool in so bravely going out to engage the enemy who were in such overwhelming force ... Their conduct has fully maintained the best traditions of the British Navy. [39]

Yet the Admiralty could not escape some censure. The Scarborough Coroner had also asked 'where was the Navy?' - a question that was echoed in many quarters. *The Times* initially adopted an impartial attitude. In its leader of 17 December, it stated that German raids against unfortified coastal towns were not difficult to accomplish but were 'devoid of military significance'. [40] But two days later, it was more critical, 'The public are not in the least alarmed, but they are puzzled. They cannot understand why a German squadron was able to reach our shores, and they understand still less how it was able to get back'. [41]

The Admiralty could not, of course, defend itself with the full truth about the sequence of events in the North Sea, for the secret of Room 40 had to be maintained. Churchill later wrote:

> We could not say a word in explanation. We had to bear in silence the censures of our countrymen. We could never admit for fear of compromising our secret information where our squadrons were, or how near the German raiding cruisers had been to their destruction. [42]

Both Fisher and Jellicoe were angered by Hipper's escape and Beatty experienced profound depression at the lost opportunity to destroy the First Scouting Group. 'If we had got them Wednesday, as we ought to have done, we should have finished the war from a naval point of view'. [43]

The failure of the Royal Navy to intercept

The German armoured cruiser, *Blucher*. 17,250 tons deep load, 530ft 6 in x 80ft 3in x 28ft 6in at deep load, and armed with twelve 21cm (8.2in) guns, eight 15cm (5.9in) guns, sixteen 8.8cm (3.45 in) guns and four 45cm (17.7in)torpedo tubes. She had a main armoured belt of 7 inches, a maximum speed of 24.25 knots, and a complement of 847 men. Q22315

The German battlecruiser *Moltke*. 25,300 tons deep load, 611ft 1in x 96ft 10ins x 29ft 5ins mean at deep load, armed with ten 28cm (11.1 inch) guns (5 x 2), twelve 15cm (5.9in), twelve 8.8cm (3.45in), and four 50cm (19.7in) torpedo tubes. Main armoured belt of 10.7in, maximum speed 25.5 knots, and a complement of 1,053. SP2700

The German battlecruiser *Von der Tann*. This ship was the first German battlecruiser. She displaced 21,700 tons (deep load), was 563ft 4in x 87ft 3in x 29ft 8in deep load. She was armed with eight 28cm (11.1 inch) guns (4 x 2), ten 15cm (5.9 inch), sixteen 8.8cm (3.45in) and four 45cm (17.7in) torpedo tubes. She had a 10 inch main armoured belt, a maximum speed of 25 knots, and a complement of 1.023 men. Q41288

The German battlecruiser *Seydlitz*. 28,100 tons deep load, 658ft x 93ft 6in x 30ft 3in at deep load. Armed with ten 28cm (11.1 inch) guns, twelve 15cm (5.9in) guns, twelve 8.8cm (3.45in) and four 50cm (19.7in) torpedo tubes. She had a main armoured belt of 12 inches, a maximum speed of 26.5 knots and a complement of 1,068 men. Q19304

Hipper's squadron can be attributed mainly to its faulty communication systems. Room 40 was still in the early stages of its development and its decoders wrongly interpreted the extent of the *Hochseeflotte's* sortie: ship-to-ship communications were unreliable or inadequate; and the Royal Navy was operating in the North Sea with its notoriously unpredictable weather and visibility. Nevertheless, it is difficult to fault the Official Historian's sombre verdict that: 'In all the war there is perhaps no action which gives deeper cause for reflection on the conduct of operations at sea'. [44]

Although some Royal Navy officers were reprimanded, the main change was the redeployment of Beatty's First Battle Cruiser Squadron and the First Light Cruiser Squadron from Cromarty to Rosyth on 21 December 1914. Rosyth became, for the remainder of the war, the main base for the battlecruisers which were, in effect, an autonomous fleet subordinate only to Jellicoe. The Admiralty maintained its concentration of the Grand Fleet in northern bases and its policy of the distant blockade.

The Imperial German Navy was also disappointed. Hipper was enraged by the premature withdrawal of von Ingenohl's capital ships which resulted both in the lost opportunity to punish the isolated British battle squadrons, and the hazardous exposure of the First Scouting Group. Von Ingenohl was criticised, too, by the Kaiser for the missed opportunity but retained his command.

Yet within the imposing framework of grand strategy, national rivalries and the clash of great navies, lies the real and personal suffering of the men, women and children of Hartlepool, Scarborough and Whitby, and the death and wounds arbitrarily inflicted upon them in the early morning of Wednesday 16 December 1914. Far greater horrors and destruction were to ensue in the years of conflict that followed, but the killing of innocent English civilians in their homes by the action of a hostile Great Power shocked the people of Britain. The prophetic denunciation of the German Navy's dawn attack in *The Times* leader of 17 December reflected the national mood:

> On the frontiers of India the tribesmen have a saying which runs. 'The patience of the British is as long as a summer day, but their arm is as long as a winter night'. The German Navy and the German nation will learn the full significance of this saying before the war is ended. [45]

The long arm of the British reached out for the *Blucher* at the Battle of the Dogger Bank on 24 January 1915. Hit by two torpedoes and fifty shells she sank with colours flying. *Seydlitz* was badly damaged. At the Battle of Jutland, 31 May – 1 June 1916, *Moltke, Von der Tann, Derfflinger* and *Seydlitz* were damaged in various degrees, the latter nearly succumbing to hits from one torpedo, eight 15-inch, six 13.5-inch, and eight 12-inch shells. [46]

The Royal Navy suffered greater losses at Jutland than the High Seas Fleet but the battle was not immediately decisive. Britain maintained her 'command of the seas' and the tightening grip of the distant blockade of Germany and its people. The High Seas Fleet's 'trailing the coat' tactics, such as the raid on the east coast ports, had failed to erode the numerical superiority of the Grand Fleet's capital ships. Unless the High Seas Fleet could fight its way out into the world's oceans and allow the import of the vital raw materials and foodstuffs - which Jutland showed it could not - Germany increasingly suffered on the economic rack.

Finally, in the last days of October 1918 the High Seas Fleet mutinied, its men driven beyond endurance by the boredom of inaction, the rigid *Kastengeist* (caste spirit) of their officers, appalling food, and deteriorating conditions at home. and, not least, by the plan devised by Grand Admiral Reinhard von Scheer, the Chief of the War Staff [47] and Hipper of a last 'death ride' by the High Seas Fleet in a climactic fight to a finish with the Grand Fleet in the North Sea. The crews, conscious of the continuing peace negotiations, rejected the Admirals' concept of an honourable *Götterdämmerung* and refused to sail in accordance with Hipper's orders. The red flag quickly replaced the Imperial eagle at the mastheads of the High Seas Fleet. On 11 November, the Armistice came into effect.

Ten days later the High Seas Fleet surrendered and to meet it were 370 ships of the Grand Fleet on their last great sortie. The light cruiser HMS *Cardiff* led the German capital ships in line astern headed by the battlecruisers *Seydlitz* (flag), *Moltke, Derfflinger, Hindenburg* and *Von der Tann*. [48] It was a little less than four years since four of these battlecruisers had bombarded Whitby, Scarborough and Hartlepool. But now the long arm of the British held them fast.

The High Seas Fleet dropped anchor at Scapa and at 1100 Admiral Sir David Beatty, Commander-in-Chief, Grand Fleet, signalled:

'The German Flag will be hauled down at sunset today, Thursday, and will not be hoisted again without permission'. [49]

On 7 May 1919, the terms of the Versailles Treaty were presented to the German delegation in Paris. In particular, the crews of the interned High Seas Fleet quickly learned that their ships were to be handed over to the victorious Allies, with Great Britain taking 70 per cent of the vessels. The officers and men realised that the ships of the *Hochseeflotte* would never return home and, even more ominously, that the Armistice was due to expire at noon on 21 June 1919.

Yet plans devised by Vice-Admiral Ludwig von Reuter, commanding the interned ships, and his officers for the scuttling of the High Seas Fleet were already well advanced. At 1120 on 21 June 1919 Reuter gave the order to scuttle and immediately seacocks and watertight doors were opened throughout the ships. At 1216 *Friederich der Grosse* sank to be followed by the *Konig Albert, Moltke* and *Seydlitz*. By 1700 all five battlecruisers, ten out of eleven battleships, four out of eight cruisers and thirty-two out of fifty destroyers had been scuttled at Scapa Flow.

Throughout the First World War the maintenance of the distant blockade and the 'command of the seas' had been the fulcrum of Allied grand strategy. As in classic Greek tragedy, nemesis follows hubris, so it was entirely fitting that the High Seas Fleet, the pride of Imperial Germany, should meet its ultimate fate under the waters of Scapa Flow, the base of the Grand Fleet, the Central Powers' most formidable enemy, and the linchpin of Great Britain's and her Allies' victory in the Great War.

Notes

1. Special Correspondent, 'After the Bombardment: A Night Visit to Hartlepool', *The Sphere*, 26 December 1914, Vol LIX, No.779.

2. A Marder, *From the Dreadnought to Scapa Flow, Vol I, The Road to War 1904 - 1914*, Oxford University Press, London, 1961, p420.

3. G Bennett, *Naval Battles of the First World War*, Batsford, London, 1968, pp 86-112.

4. J Goldrick, *The Kings Ships were at Sea*, Tri-Service Press Ltd, Annapolis, 1984, pp 190-191.

5. Goldrick, op cit, p l90.

6. This information is from three sources:
(i) P Beesly, *Room 40: British Naval Intelligence 1914-18*, Hamish Hamilton, London, 1982, pp 1-7.
(ii) J Goldrick, op cit, pp 176-177.
(iii) D Kahn, *Seizing the Enigma: The Race to Break the German U-Boat Codes 1939-1943*, Souvenir Press, London, 1991, pp 15-30.

7. Beesly, op cit, p 51.

8. Beesly, op cit, p 51.

9. Goldrick, op cit, pp 193-194.

10. The account of the movements of the High Seas Fleet, Royal Navy warships and the German bombardments relies heavily on two main primary sources. Public Records Office ADM 137/1943 and ADM 137/2084, referred to in the notes as PRO ADM.
Also three main secondary sources:
i) J Corbett, *History of the Great War, Naval Operations Vol II*, Longman, Green & Co, 1921, London, p 23-46.
(ii) Goldrick, op cit, pp 193-209.
(iii) A Marder, *From the Dreadnought to Scapa Flow: Vol 2 The War Years to the Eve of Jutland 1914-16*, Oxford University Press, London, 1965, p135-142.

11. Corbett, op cit, p 22. Marder, op cit., p 36.

12. Corbett, op cit, p 22.

13. PRO/ADM and Goldrick, op cit, p l98.

14. Corbett, op cit, p 32.

15. *The Illustrated London News*, 26 December 1914, Vol CXLV, No 949, pp·864-865.

16. *The Times*, 17 December 1914.

17. D Chandler, 'The Bombardment of the East Coast', *History of the First World War*, Vol 2 No 23, Purnell, 1970, p 264.

18. PRO/ADM and Goldrick, op cit, pp 200-210.

19. PRO/ADM and Goldrick, op cit, p 200.

20. Department of Documents, papers of Mr W N Collins. 66/104/1,

Eyewitness account of the bombardment of Hartlepool, 16 December 1914. Further quoted as the Collins Papers.

21. The Mk7 fired a 100-lb. projectile to a maximum range of 12,000 yards. I V Hogg and L F Thurston, *British Artillery Weapons and Ammunitions 1914-18*, Ian Allan, London, 1972, pp 130-131.

22. Collins Papers.

23. Department of Documents, papers of Captain E C Brent RN, P464 'Patrol Flotilla engagement during the bombardment of Hartlepool by German Battlecruisers on 16 December 1914'. Further quoted as the Brent Papers.

24. Brent Papers.

25. PRO/ADM.

26. Goldrick, op cit, p 201.

27. Collins Papers.

28. Collins Papers.

29. D Chandler, op cit, p 624.

30. PRO/ADM.

31. PRO/ADM Marder, Vol 111, op cit, pp 137-138.

32. W Churchill, *The World Crisis 1911-1918, Vol 1*, Odhams Press Ltd, 1938, p 419.

33. B M Ranft, *The Beatty Papers*, Scolar Press, London, 1989, pp 181-182.

34. Marder, Vol 11, op cit, pp 141-142.

35. D Chandler, op cit, p 25.

36. *The Times*, 17 December, 1914.

37. *The Times*, 17 December, 1914.

38. *The Times*, 19 December, 1914.

39. Brent Papers.

40. *The Times*, 17 December, 1914.

41. *The Times*, 19 December, 1914.

42. Churchill, op cit, p 429.

43. W S Chalmers, *The Life and Letters of David, Earl Beatty, Admiral of the Fleet*, Hodder and Stoughton, London, 1951, p 75. From a letter from Beatty to Lady Beatty, 20 December 1914.

44. Corbett, op. cit., p 43.

45. *The Times*, 17 December, 1914.

46. R Gardiner (ed), *Conway's All the World's Fighting Ships 1906-1921*, Conway Maritime Press, London, 1985, pp 150-155.

47. H H Herwig, *The German Naval Officer Corps: A Social and Political History 1890-1918*, Oxford University press, Oxford, 1973, pp 255-265.

48. J Costello and T Hughes, *Jutland 1916*, Futura Publications Ltd, London, 1976, p 231.

49. A J Marder, *From the Dreadnought to Scapa Flow, Vol V. Victory and Aftermath (January 1918-June 1919)*, Oxford University Press, London, 1970, p 191.

Further Reading

H H Herwig, *Luxury Fleet: The Imperial German Navy 1888-1918*, George Allen and Unwin, London, 1980.

D Kahn, *The Code-Breakers*, Weidenfeld and Nicolson, London, 1966.

R F Mackay, *Fisher of Silverstone*, Clarendon Press, Oxford, 1973.

The Imperial War Museum

The Imperial War Museum illustrates and records all aspects of the two world wars and other military operations involving Britain and the Commonwealth since 1914. The Museum, founded in 1917, was established by Act of Parliament in 1920 and has been in its present home (formerly the Bethlem Royal Hospital or Bedlam) since 1936. The Museum has three branches, HMS *Belfast*, Duxford and the Cabinet War Rooms. The Museum also occupies the former All Saints' Hospital, close to the Main Building, which houses a number of reference departments.

Research and Study Facilities

The Museum welcomes approaches from members of the public for research and study purposes. Its resources cover not only naval, military and air operations but also the social, political, economic and artistic aspects of conflict in the twentieth century.

Visitors intending to use the Museum's reference facilities should be aware that material of relevance to their fields of study may be found in more than one of the departments listed below. Separate leaflets describing the holdings of the departments and the services they offer are available on request.

Department of Art: responsible for the Museum's paintings, drawings and sculptures, and for its collections of posters, medallions and postcards. The Department also has a unique collection of correspondence with artists who were commissioned under the war artist scheme in the two world wars.

Department of Documents: primary source material, largely composed of British private papers and captured German records. It includes the papers of high-ranking officers such as Field Marshals Sir John French, Sir Henry Wilson and Viscount Montgomery of Alamein, manuscripts of the war poets and writers Isaac Rosenberg and Siegfried Sassoon and many personal diaries, letters and unpublished memoirs.

Department of Exhibits and Firearms: administers the Museum's collections of three-dimensional objects. Besides such larger exhibits as aircraft, artillery, vehicles and small craft, most of which are displayed at Duxford near Cambridge, the holdings include uniforms, insignia, weapons, flags, communications equipment, models, medical equipment, cameras, toys, currency and ephemera.

Department of Film: holds more than forty million feet of film. Apart from material shot by service cameramen and films sponsored by the service ministries and the Ministry of Information, there are substantial holdings from other Allied and enemy sources, as well as many important documentaries, television compilations and feature films.

Department of Photographs: a national archive of some five million photographs which includes the work of official military, professional and private photographers. Guides to various areas of the collection include a concise catalogue covering the First and Second World Wars. Lists of photographs on specific subjects are available and a catalogue of their titles can be sent on request.

Department of Printed Books: a national reference library comprising over 100,000 books as well as extensive collections of pamphlets, periodicals, maps and technical drawings. In addition the Department holds important special collections including those on women's activities during the First World War, aerial propaganda leaflets and ephemera such as song-sheets, stamps and theatre programmes.

Department of Sound Records: over 15,000 hours of recorded material, retrospective interviews with service personnel and civilians, contemporary archive recordings including speeches by well known personalities, war reports and broadcasts, sound effects and war crimes trials; and miscellaneous recordings such as radio programmes, lectures and poetry readings.

Opening hours

Reference Departments
Monday to Friday 10.00 am to 5.00 pm

At least 24 hours' notice should be given of an intended visit (for a visit to the Department of Art at least 48 hours' notice, and for the Department of Film at least one week's notice is necessary).

Saturday 10.00 am to 5.00 pm

Departments of Documents and Printed Books only. A restricted service is offered on Saturday (except Bank Holiday weekends and the last two weekends of November). An appointment is essential since only pre-booked material can be made available and there is limited seating.

The Reference Departments are closed on Bank Holidays. The Departments of Documents and Printed Books are closed for the last two full weeks in November.

Imperial War Museum, Lambeth Road
London SE1 6HZ 071-416 5000

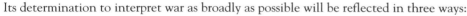